THERE IS A LIGHT THAT SHINES

A SPIRITUAL AUTOBIOGRAPHY

by Rory B. Mackay

"There is a light that shines
beyond all things on earth,
beyond us all, beyond the heavens,
the very highest heavens–
The light that shines in our Heart."

– Chandogya Upanishad, 3.13.7

This work is licensed under a Creative Commons Attribution 4.0 International license. This license allows for redistribution, commercial and non-commercial, provided the author is credited and no modifications are made to the material. For contract details, visit https://creativecommons.org/licenses/by-nd/4.0/

Copyright © 2023 Rory B. Mackay, some rights reserved.

First edition

Published by Blue Star Publishing

UnbrokenSelf.com

The right of Rory B. Mackay to be identified as the author of this work has been asserted by him in accordance with the Copyright, Designs and Patents Act, 1988.

There Is A Light That Shines / Rory B. Mackay — 1st ed.

ISBN 978-1-7396089-4-1

Dedication
For my Mother, whose light and love kindled the spiritual fire that transformed my life.

Contents

Introduction	–i

Part 1: Becoming a Person
A World Appears	–1
Enter, Ego	–7
A Tale of Two Neighbours	–15
A Young Misfit	–19
Everything Changes	–29
Being a Teenager	–35
Thank Goodness It's Not Just Me	–45
A Greater Reality	–49
The Pendulum Swings	–55
Dance of Duality	–59
Unwitting Sannyasi	–65

Part 2: The Flame Ignites
More to Life	–73
The Motivation Behind Spiritual Seeking	–77
Truths and Half-Truths	–83
A Spiritual Treasure Trail	–87
I Am That	–91
Day of Bliss	–95

Part 3: Vedanta - Map to Freedom
How to Attain Enlightenment	–103
Vedanta	–107
I Meet My Guru	–113
The Highest Blessing	–121
I Found My Purpose	–127
Airport Epiphany	–133
I Got It, I Lost It	–143
The Spiritual Achilles Heel	–147
Relationships and the Love Issue	–151
A Matter of Commitment	–161
Karma Yoga and a Life of Service	–167
A Trip to India	–171
Chasing Spiritual Highs	–181
Self-Realised or Certifiable?	–187

No Enlightenment Certificate	−193
Some Spiritual Misconceptions	−201
Nothing to Get From the World	−207

Part 4: Dharma, Duty and Freedom Amid Adversity

We Each Have a Dharma to Fulfil	−213
A Writer's Story	−207
A Dream and a Question	−223
The Teacher is a Mirror	−229
Satisfaction Guaranteed	−237
Karma	−245
A Dream of Dark and Light	−251
My Arjuna Moment	−257
Dispassion and Dharma of the Body	−263
Judgement, Compassion and Understanding	−269
There Is No Death	−275
The Ultimate Aim of All Spiritual Teaching	−279
A Free Mind	−283
Savour Each Day	−289
A Meditation on Awareness	−297
A Meditation on Jiva	−301
What I've Learned in Life	−303
Be Free	−309
Further Reading and Listening	−313

THERE IS A LIGHT THAT SHINES

"Everyone has the right to tell the truth about his or her own life."

Ellen Bass

Introduction

A couple of years ago, I met up with a friend I hadn't seen for the best part of a decade. We grabbed a coffee and strolled around Edinburgh's Princes Street Gardens, catching up on news and discussing where our lives had taken us since last we'd met. I listened with interest as he talked about the ups and downs of his career and spoke about a recent breakup before discussing his plans for the future.

When it came turn to talk about myself, I realised that a significant amount of my life those past few years had been devoted to my spiritual journey. In fact, it had become impossible to separate my life, and who I was as a person, from the spiritual fire in my heart.

His immediate reaction was priceless: "Oh, cool, so you're still into your Buddhist shit?"

I just smiled. Of course, I wouldn't have described it as either specifically "Buddhist" or "shit", but, for the uninitiated, that was probably as good a description as any.

I couldn't deny that spirituality had been an integral part of my life since my teens and had become more so as the years progressed. This isn't something easily understood by the majority of people. The desire, or, in my case, the imperative, to seek answers about the nature of the Self and Reality is not one shared by the average worldly person. Why would it be when most people are too busy getting on with the basics of material life, juggling careers, marriage and kids as they focus on what Vedic tradition outlines as the first three goals of human life: security, pleasure and virtue.

I'd wager that few have any idea that another, higher, goal exists beyond these. The Vedic scriptures are absolutely clear, however, that there is not only a fourth pursuit, but that it qualifies as life's highest goal. This goal? Spiritual enlightenment or liberation from suffering.

While the average person is likely to see the pursuit of enlightenment as a wacky quirk at best, the spiritual impulse exists in all people. I believe it manifests as our innermost desire for wholeness, connection and lasting happiness. Unfortunately, this impulse is generally misdirected into an endlessly futile quest to extract lasting happiness and fulfilment from objects and experiences outside of ourselves.

Furthermore, when a culture does away with the spiritual, as ours certainly has, something has to fill the God-sized vacuum. It's perhaps no wonder that the human ego with its inherent need to be right and to look good, has expanded to fill the void. Along with the ascent of the ego, various worldly things are also elevated to Godlike status: whether it be money, pleasure, power or any of an infinite number of objects of desire.

None of this should come as a surprise. Our senses are naturally extroverted. This keeps our attention fixed upon the material world and ignorant of the vast and ever present inner light by which we perceive reality. On top of that, we happen to be born into a hyper-materialistic culture; one that conditions us from a young age to believe that happiness and fulfilment can only be found outside of us in the world of shiny "things".

It's not an easy spell to break. Entire lifetimes will pass before we finally concede that the solution to our suffering cannot be our continual and frustrated attempts to align the outer circumstances of our lives with our inner desires. Indeed, it's only when we've experienced the relentless pain and frustration of trying to "make it" and "be somebody" that we realise the futility of seeking permanent happiness in an impermanent world.

Whereas disillusionment leads most to bitterness and defeat, the wise person may recognise it as the very doorway to freedom. That's when, with a little luck, or grace, we come to the realisation that, contrary to everything we've been told, life isn't about getting what we want. Life is about breaking free from want and discovering the part of us that is without desire; the part of us already whole, complete and untouched by anything in this world.

This great secret of life is something only a small percentage of people ever come to realise. The full assimilation and integration of this knowledge is called enlightenment. The original Sanskrit word for it is *moksha*, which means "liberation" or "freedom"—and that, I'm sure you'll agree, is what we're all ultimately looking for.

When we come to know who and what we truly are at the deepest, most intrinsic level, everything changes. We find ourselves no longer dependent upon the world and our circumstances being a certain way in order to be happy. Indeed, a liberated person enjoys a deep and lasting happiness quite independent of external factors.

Spiritual enlightenment isn't about adopting a set of beliefs or doctrines, nor is it about supernatural beings, or attaining special powers or higher states of consciousness. It's simply the act of re-educating the mind and shifting our centre of identification from the false to the True; from the conceptual ego-self to the underlying Awareness; the Light by which we experience the entire universe.

That's what this book is about; nothing more, nothing less.

I have to confess I never thought in a million years I would ever write anything approximating an autobiography. I tend to be private by nature and, unlike most people, my personal story holds little interest to me.

On this occasion, however, I felt compelled to share something of my life's path told through the lens of spiritual awakening. What follows is far from a complete autobiography. It's more a curation of vignettes: events, experiences and, most importantly, the knowledge gained by them. Like pearls on a string, they are linked by a common thread: finding an end to suffering through Self-Realisation.

While the initial part of the book is obviously specific to my early experiences in life, it leads into a far greater, more impersonal and universal subject matter; one that relates not just to the person writing these words, but to the person reading them; and, indeed, everyone walking this timeless path to Self-Knowledge.

Friends and family members may naturally be eager to see what I've written about them. In all likelihood, I haven't written about them at all—not because they aren't important to me, but because they are, and I believe that relationships are personal. That's why I've generally only included the people and events that have a direct connection to my spiritual journey and the events precipitating it.

In Song of Myself, Walt Whitman declared, "I am large, I contain multitudes." Human beings are complex and messy, often filled with competing and contradictory impulses and imperatives. Looking back, I see myself as no different. In an effort to streamline and avoid self-indulgence, I've left out parts of my life which had no relevance to the overarching theme. Unless you have an existing interest or openness with regard to spiritual awakening, you probably won't find this book particularly interesting or comprehensible. Like my good friend, you'll probably just think of it as weird "Buddhist shit", which is fair enough.

In actuality, the key subject matter is not Buddhism, but Vedanta; the ancient school of spiritual knowledge rooted in the Vedas (from which Buddhism itself is an offshoot). It would be impossible to write about my life without including Vedanta in significant detail. Indeed, to borrow the words of the renowned 19th century philosopher Arthur Schopenhauer, "Vedanta has been the solace of my life, and it will be the solace of my death."

This isn't, however, a book on the nuts and bolts of Vedanta. While I have filled in some of the basics, it's less a book on Vedantic theory and more a book on Vedantic practise; and, specifically, how I took this teaching, lived it and made it work for me. For an introduction and overview of the key principles, I suggest another book I intend to release more or less simultaneously with this, titled "Enlightenment Made Simple: An Introduction to Advaita Vedanta." You'll find more recommended resources at the "Further Reading" appendix.

The book is written not so much in chapters as short sections, because that's really the only way I was able to get through such an immense project. As with all autobiographies, there's no real end, and, God willing, I may add the odd update for subsequent editions. It's been hard knowing quite what to include and what not to include. I'm reminded of the REM lyrics "Oh no, I've said too much / I haven't said enough". Ultimately, I've approach this task with a mixture of dispassion and compassion and I can only hope I've managed to strike the right balance.

Again, I want to stress that this book was written not to cast a spotlight on Rory, the person. That wouldn't be of interest to many people. What you'll find is something of an oxymoron: an ultimately transpersonal autobiography. It's about a lifelong spiritual quest that took me from wounded seeker to contented finder—by revealing that the problematic person I thought I was wasn't even real in the first place!

Maybe I should put up a spoiler warning here, but the crux of what I learned is this: Everything that I ever wanted and sought, and all of the joy, fulfilment and love and validation I desperately craved from the world and from others, already existed within me as the very core of my being. Fortunately, it's not just my being, but yours too, for, in spite of appearances, we are all the same—many faces reflecting a single universal Consciousness.

I share this as an act of love, in the hope it will be of help and inspiration to all sincere spiritual seekers. This is for anyone who knows that there is more to Reality than appearance alone, and for those yearn to be free of the bondage of ego-based limitation and its all-consuming whirlpool of fear, desire and attachment.

Think of this as an invitation to embrace your birthright and uncover the boundless ocean of love and joy at the very core of your being. This isn't just my story. It's ultimately your story, too, and, to that end, I dedicate this book from my heart to yours and to the Light that shines within us all.

Part 1

BECOMING A PERSON

"Life is too short to be little."

Benjamin Disraeli

A World Appears

According to conventional understanding, we are each born into the world. At a certain time and place, a baby appears; usually in a hospital bed and courtesy of our mother, father and, most likely, a team of doctors and nurses.

I was no different, although I have to take my parents' word for that.

In my own direct experience, I didn't appear in the world on the 25th of January 1979. Rather, the world appeared in me; in my consciousness. I never had the sense of not-existing prior to that, nor I can't pinpoint a time when I suddenly came into being. There was just consciousness; and, at some point, a body and entire world appeared in that consciousness.

Over the successive weeks and months, this little baby-form became aware of various impressions; of my mother and father, of the house we lived in, my cherished Pooh Bear and the various sights and sounds appearing in my awareness, only a few of which I can recollect with any clarity. Whether I appeared in the world or the world appeared in me, there was, nevertheless, a new kid on the block; his name, Rory Binnie Mackay (the surname is pronounced Mac-Aye, for what it's worth).

While it's fashionable these days to blame our childhood and upbringing for just about anything wrong in our lives, I look back upon my childhood with nothing but fondness and gratitude. Without a doubt, I was blessed with a good birth, being born into a family that provided me with immense love, support and stability. I will forever be grateful for that gift of life and, more importantly, the gift of love.

Unfortunately, I don't think I was particularly appreciative at the time. I'm told that I was not an easy child during my first couple of years. In fact, by all accounts, I seemed to enter this world in a disturbed and unhappy state, constantly crying and refusing to feed or settle. At one point, the doctor decided to run a raft of tests just to make sure there wasn't something wrong with me medically.

The malady wasn't physical, however. I was just an unhappy baby. I later learned that I came into this world carrying past karmic trauma and I think that may have been why, at some deep, unconscious level, I didn't particularly want to be here. Indeed, for much of my life, I never felt quite at home in this world.

As it happens, I was born during the so-called Winter of Discontent; a time of widespread political, social and economic upheaval in the UK, with strikes left, right and centre, daily power cuts and shortages of basic amenities. The Glasgow hospital where I was born was very much affected by the chaos and experienced regular power cuts and lacked even such basics as bedsheets (instead making do with paper sheets). My birth hadn't been an easy one and was, according to my mother, rather chaotic and traumatic. The moment I was born, I was separated from my mother and kept apart for the first twenty four hours. That definitely isn't ideal for a newborn baby or mother and undoubtedly contributed to my distressed state.

In spite of my tears, tantrums and hunger strike, my mother nurtured me with endless patience and love, even though it took a toll on her own physical and emotional health. My mother is without doubt one of the kindest, most caring and empathetic human beings I have ever encountered in this world; someone who automatically puts others before herself and gives of herself without question and limit. I believe that, unless a person's personality and emotional issues interfere, as they sadly do for some, a mother's love is perhaps as close to divine love as you might find on earth; a love that is pure, unconditional and inexhaustible. I am certain I wouldn't have survived long without the unending care and love of my mother.

My parents happened to have very different temperaments and this often resulted in an environment with conflict; something I would find difficult being the highly sensitive child I was. My father was of steadfast support, providing security and stability from the moment I can remember. Unlike my mother, he was of a more introverted, distant nature; personality traits I would later recognise in myself too. His parenting style reflected his own childhood and would definitely be classed as more "old school", for it was altogether less demonstrative and accompanied by an often forbidding temper. Years later, I would come to see that people are wired differently; that each person has a different capacity to express love and affection; and that this is not at all a reflection upon our own worth or worthiness to receive love. That realisation would, in time, lead to a closer relationship and I'm forever grateful that, like my mother, my father was there for me like a rock through all the ups and downs of my, at times, turbulent passage through life.

Two years after I was born, I was joined by a baby sister. I can vaguely remember the shock to my system when, after a lengthy absence, Mum reappeared from hospital one day with a younger model. While we often wound each other up as only siblings can, Holly and I developed a close bond as we grew up together; one that remains to this day. I feel blessed that my family, including my grandparents, whom I adored beyond words, gifted me with such a marvellous upbringing.

My sister and I were brought up to have kindness, class, empathy and a love for animals, nature and all of life. These are truly valuable traits to instil in a child. While the greater part of who we become is determined by the karmic blueprint of the causal body, we are also, in many ways, a product of our environment and upbringing. For that, I am eternally grateful that my sister and I were raised to be caring, compassionate and spiritually minded human beings.

Speaking of spirituality, my parents were raised Protestant and we went to Church every Sunday. I have to confess that, as a child, Church was nothing but a drudgery (and one that seemed a terrible waste of time on one of only two days off school!). The stories and sermons the minister delivered each week didn't mean much to me. I was, however, always fascinated and inwardly enthralled by the concept of God; something I didn't understand but which I was, nevertheless, readily able to accept.

I can remember having conversations with my Mum at a very young age, asking where God was and how we were related to Him. I recall Mum trying to explain that we all have a "spirit"; an innermost part of our being that existed within yet beyond the body. I could instinctively take that on board, even if my undeveloped mind struggled with the abstract nature of it. While my Dad wasn't particularly interested in religion or spiritual matters beyond social obligation, Mum was blessed by a deep and genuine spirituality; a faith and openness which influenced me profoundly. It ignited a spark within me; a spark that, in time, became a fire that would light my life throughout the years to follow.

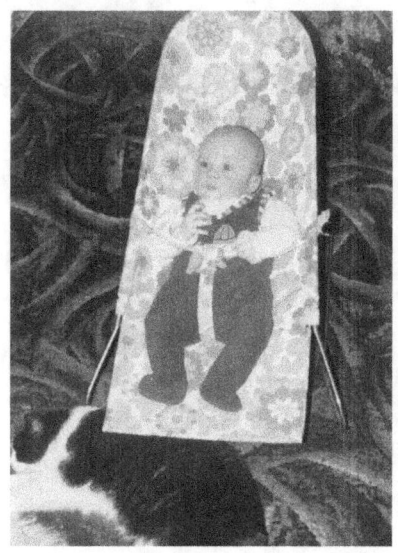
Aged 4-5 months with cat Penny

With Mum at my very first Christmas

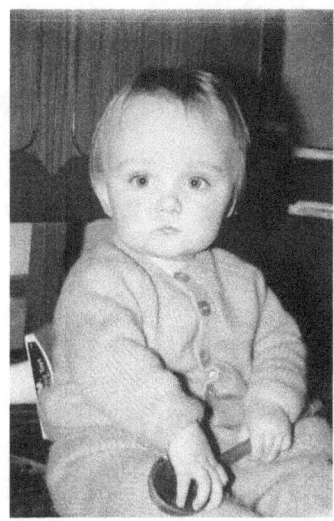

Above: Looking reflective even at 12 months old.
Right: My little sister Holly arrives.

"God shines everywhere in stone and earth and water, but men who have not overcome their ego fail to find the Resplendent One anywhere."

Swami Tapovan

Enter, Ego

Assuming we've been blessed with good parents and a stable, loving environment, our first few years in this world are, in some ways, probably our easiest. While there's a heck of a lot of growth and development taking place both physically and cognitively, one of the things that takes time to develop is the ego; the sense of being a separate and autonomous being.

I'd wager that one of the reasons people tend to love babies is that babies exist in a pre-ego state. Unencumbered by a sense of self, all we see is Awareness shining in all its purity, unfiltered by the mental overlay of concepts and conditioning; which will, in time, drive a wedge between us and the apprehension of our own true nature.

Along with animals, young children reflect something that virtually all human adults seem to lose in themselves: namely, the purity and simplicity of just *being*; the sense of existing but not existing as "this" or "that". For an infant, there's nothing to be or become, or to achieve or prove. There's simply the light of Consciousness shining through form; completely unmanufactured, uncontrived and free from any shadow of self-doubt. That, alas, will come with time.

My earliest memories in this life are just snippets without any linking narrative. I remember my mother holding and calming me when I was crying, and I can recall my first bedroom and looking out of the bars of my cot. Maybe I'm crazy, but I swear I can still remember the sense of strangeness that I was somehow tethered to a body, a form, and surrounded by all these other forms. It felt alien to me at some deep, instinctual level; constrictive and strange. What *was* this place, and why I was here?

I can vividly recall gazing out of my bedroom window one night, when I was perhaps only two years old. It had been snowing and I stood marvelling at the orange glow of the street lamps upon the silken blanket of snow covering the road, pavement and houses. I'd never laid eyes upon snow before and it was a thing of magic.

For no particular reason, I also remember being in the back garden another day with my father, eating a tube of Smarties (a type of sugar-coated chocolate drop) and feeling really accomplished that I had mastered the art of eating more than one at a time. My Dad, less impressed, told me that if I only ate one a time they'd last longer. What conundrums life could pose, even at such a tender age.

I can still see Mum serving me toast soldiers with a boiled egg for lunch, while the television news was on in the background with presenter Moira Stewart recounting the events of the day with her most distinctive and dulcet of voices.

I recall another day when my Grandfather took my sister and I for a walk to a nearby stream (or "burn" as we can them in Scotland). We stood watching a mother duck and her babies as they happily accepted crumbs of bread. It was a misty day, and the fields and bare limbed trees were only partly visible through the haze. I don't think I'd ever seen mist or fog before. Like the first snowfall, it obviously left a lasting impression in my young mind.

Another earliest of memories is the house filled with family members after my sister's Christening and playing around with pots and pans in the kitchen and my Grandfather calling me "Baker Mackay". Even as a toddler, I had an interest in making food. It would become a lifelong hobby and something I'd get rather good at, too—although, obviously, it would be a number of years before I'd be capable of doing anything productive in the kitchen (aside from almost burning it down; but that's a whole other story).

Christmas always seemed a magical time back then, with lights, decorations, a tree and, best of all for a young kid—presents! One of my first Christmases, I was given a toy kitchen by Santa, filled with pots and pans and all kinds of utensils. It was of little practical use when it came to making food, of course, but I loved it and it was a good enough start for this eager young chef.

These memories are unaccompanied by any particular sense of "self". There was just Awareness experiencing a succession of sights, sounds and events at certain points in time and space. Eventually, however, the sense of being a separate self, a "person"—in my case called Rory—would develop over the course of several years.

For there's a certain point when we're growing up and our mind and psyche taking shape that we experience a sense of contraction in our being. The vastness, openness and wonder that we experienced so effortlessly as a young child begins to contract and coalesce into a far narrower sense of identity. Duality comes into being and, along with it, the contrasting notions of "self" and "other". The root cause of this may be what neuroscientists refer to as the left-brain interpreter; a function of the mind and ego which divides reality into "me" and "the world", "good" versus "bad" and, even worse, "how I am" versus "how I should be."

Over time, bit by bit, we become locked into the sense of being a separate and autonomous individual; the ego, or "self" (with the little "s"). Whereas before everything seemed interconnected and non-separate from us, we now begin viewing ourselves as disconnected and distinct from our environment and from other people.

I can't remember in any real detail how I came to believe that I was an ego; a person with a name, age and a particular identity. Obviously, my parents named me Rory, a label I accepted, as we all do (apart from my sister, who, strong willed from an early age, decided to rename herself aged two; but she is a rare exception!).

Because we know so little at that age, we rely upon our parents and other authority figures to tell us who and what we are. Unfortunately, unless we happen to be born to extremely advanced, enlightened parents who see us as pure Awareness animating a body and mind, you can guarantee they're going to teach us that we are an ego self; a little person-in-the-making.

Tragically, the moment we come to believe the fiction that we are a body/mind/ego self, we begin to lose touch with the vast, undefined openness that we experienced in the pre-ego state. We become locked into identification with name and form and seemingly estranged from our own nature. That's simply the way it goes.

The ego is both our blessing and curse. Our ability to conceive of ourselves as autonomous beings and to self-reflect has, for better or worse, enabled us to become the dominant species on the planet. While certain animals have a rudimentary sense of self, none would seem to possess the human being's advanced capacity for self-reflection and self-determination. It would seem that the ego, the sense of being a distinct entity with certain likes and dislikes, values, desires and ambitions, is key to our functioning in the world in an effective capacity.

The downside to this enhanced capacity for self-evaluation is clear. While it's possible we might decide that the "self" we think we are is fine as it is, it's just as likely, if not more so, that we judge ourselves as being *not* good enough in some way; as being somehow insufficient, flawed or defective.

The inevitable consequence of such a negative self-evaluation? An entire lifetime spent trying to "fix" ourselves any way we can.

The brain comes equipped with a negativity bias; a mechanism which, rather perversely, is actually designed to keep us safe. If it perceives something wrong, it will divert as much attention to the problem as possible in the hope we will take notice and fix it. So, if we happen to judge ourselves as flawed and deficient as a human being, you can bet that the mind won't let up on it. Moreover, it's likely to become a defining factor of our entire experience of living. Such neurosis is strictly the purview of human beings. You'll never find a goldfish or a cat that thinks it's not good enough and must somehow find a way to compensate for its inherent "brokenness".

Of course, we're not born like this. When we're babies, we don't have many expectations put upon us. We eat, sleep, gurgle and poop and it's all seen as adorable. By the time we become toddlers, driven by the instinctual dynamism of what Freud called the "id", the scaffolding around the burgeoning ego has been installed and work commenced on it in earnest.

As we begin developing a more cohesive sense of self, we become aware that the approval of those around us is no longer unconditional. We find that certain behaviours and actions are encouraged and praised and others are prohibited and may elicit our caregivers' disapproval or even anger. These prohibitions are invariably for our own well-being and safety, although we might not appreciate that at the time.

We learn to become hyper-vigilant of our environment and to the cues of those around us. We're not only now aware of being a separate self, but we have to fight to protect the integrity of that self. After all, the love and validation of adults depends on whether we are deemed "good" or "bad", so there's now a danger that we might lose that approval. As children, we are utterly dependent upon our caregivers, so this fear—the possibility that somehow we might not be good enough to be loved—can be genuinely terrifying.

As a result, the ego assumes control and a world of defence mechanisms and obfuscations are born. This, as much as anything, sows the seed of what we call samsara; the whirlpool of existential suffering that has blighted our species since the very inception of the human ego. The first step is when we come to see ourselves as a separate person. We then self-reflect and judge the person we see ourselves as being deficient in some way. Our behaviour is then motivated by the desire to fix that broken self in order to elevate ourselves both in our own eyes and the eyes of others.

It's a sad story—particularly because, as I was to find out much later, this ego-self was never actually who we were to begin with. Our suffering is born of a lie; a case of fundamental self-misidentification. Ignorance, however, both universal and personal, blinds us so completely. That's why there comes a certain, inevitable point in every person's childhood when we lose sight of who we are, and we must then spend a lifetime trying to find ourselves again.

The inevitable consequence of such a negative self-evaluation? An entire lifetime spent trying to "fix" ourselves any way we can.

"The moon in the water,
Broken and broken again;
Still it is there."
Choshu

A Tale of Two Neighbours

My first real friend in life wasn't another kid, but our next door neighbour, a recently retired lady around the same age as my grandparents. From the moment I met her, Mary felt like family, and, although my memories are hazy, I can remember sneaking off to her house just to be around her warm and loving energy. Fortunately, she didn't mind at all and, in fact, looked forward to my visits. Having never married or had kids, Mary considered me the grandson she never had.

I guess I was a quirky little kid because I had a fixation with certain mechanical things; particularly washing machines, which, for some strange reason, fascinated me. I remember Mary would fix me a drink, get me a little seat and I would watch her washing machine as it span round and round and all seemed right with the world. Those were simpler times for sure! I'm happy that, even after my family moved away, we kept in touch with Mary and I saw her a number of times over the years including regular visits to see her around Easter time.

Of course, not everybody in life would be as kind and welcoming, as we all must come to learn at some point. I vividly recall a day when I was about three years old; certainly long before I started school. Mum was visiting another neighbour and I was happily playing in the front garden outside, the sun shining and the birds singing. Obviously, Mum was keeping an eye on me; but, so good at stealth manoeuvres was I, she didn't notice when I slipped out of the garden.

Another kid, around the same age as me, appeared on his doorstep and called me over. My memory is fuzzy on the details, but I think that I knew him from whatever preschool group we were at. Anyway, thinking nothing of it, I accepted his invitation and he ushered me into his house with the promise of chocolate biscuits.

We weren't doing anything wrong; just kids being kids and reaching for the biscuit tin. I can't have been in there for more than a few minutes when his mother stormed in. Clearly already in a foul mood, she was perhaps understandably shocked at seeing some random child in her house.

Unfortunately for me, her surprise manifested as a startling rage and she bellowed, **"WHAT ARE YOU DOING HERE?! GET OUT OF MY HOUSE, NOW!! GET OUT!!"**

Shocked and startled, I didn't stick around. I bolted back to the neighbours' garden. I held back my tears until I was in the garden and then I let them out full pelt. As I started crying, Mum immediately appeared, asking what was wrong.

Here's the interesting part of the story. I didn't tell her what had happened. I lied. It may or may not have been the first lie I ever told. I said that I'd just fallen over and hurt myself. Obviously there was no sign of injury, but she had no reason to doubt what I'd said. She took me inside and got me a drink and I calmed down.

The incident, however, as minor as it might seem, left a mark. It may well have been the moment I realised that I wasn't going to be welcomed with open arms by everyone; that not all places were safe and not all adults were benign and non-threatening. While I'd certainly gotten into trouble before and there were far worse things happened in my childhood, something about this experience shook me in a way that I wouldn't understand for many years to come.

Kids tend to think in a primal, instinctual way that doesn't always conform to reason or logic. I think the reason I didn't tell my mother what had happened was out of fear that I was somehow responsible for the way the woman treated me—because I was bad, or unwanted, or otherwise had something else indelibly wrong with me. Again, it's not rational, but when something happens to a child, they are inclined to think it's because of them; that they deserved it in some way. I didn't want anyone else to see me in a bad light or to react in the way the harassed neighbour woman had.

A little part of my psyche contracted that day. It didn't happen all at once, but I learned to involuntarily pull my energy inward. This became almost a reflex response in which I instinctively withdrew and hid from the world and from anyone I deemed threatening. It maybe began that day but it would be reinforced many times over the years. It's only looking back now that I can understand how I interpreted this event. I realised that I couldn't be entirely open with others; that I had to be cautious and keep certain things private. I learned to retreat into myself, to be guarded and to hide anything I thought might cast me in a bad light.

My ego had added a new self-protection subroutine. This fear of potentially being rejected and cast out was a seed that would grow with time and eventually branch into a whole forest of related beliefs and fears. As it happens, much of the rest of my life and the entirety of my spiritual search would be devoted to the overcoming of this contracted sense of self.

"Sometimes you never know the value of a moment until it becomes a memory."

Dr Seuss

A Young Misfit

Life in a world of duality is neither all good nor all bad; neither entirely happy nor entirely sad. Indeed, anyone with keen insight can see that happiness and joy are not unqualified blessings. Each are offset by equal measures of limitation and pain. Such is life in a world of contrasting opposites.

While I consider myself blessed to have been born into a loving family, my childhood wasn't always easy. As I recall, starting school was something of an ordeal. I can still remember the day Mum took me to this sprawling, unfamiliar building packed with all these other kids I didn't know; so many of whom seemed loud, brash and excitable. I was horrified when she made to leave. Why the heck would she leave me here? I didn't want to be here! I wanted to stay at home and do what I normally did. What was going on?

It didn't take long before I realised that I was something of a misfit. While most of the other kids, the boys in particular, were rambunctious live-wires, I was generally quiet and shy. The noise, stimulus and the unfamiliarity of it all were a shock to the system. I had a natural tendency to shut down in the face of it; to pull back and do my best to disengage and merge into the background. It simply wasn't my nature to push myself forward, assert myself and dominate proceedings. I immediately knew this set me apart. I felt different; somehow lacking; a sense that would stick with me for many years to come.

It wasn't until decades later that I could look back and realise that, heck, that's okay—and I was okay! I wasn't some failure as a human being just because I was shy and sensitive. I was just an *introvert!* That's simply the way I was created and, much later, I'd come to realise that this was, in many ways, actually a good thing with significant advantages—particularly spiritually.

One of the things I wish I'd known back then is that we are all born with an innate nature and personality type. We're not all meant to be the same, even if we are all trying to live up to some standardised, and generally quite impossible, ideal. Whereas some people are extroverts by nature, others tend toward introversion. Studies have shown that extroverts and introverts have differently wired brains. Whereas the latter thrive in situations where they're dealing with other people and various social interactions, introverts, after even a short time, find such situations overwhelming and exhausting. As it happens, there's no shame in that. Our brains simply process stimulation in different ways and, as the old saying goes, one man's meat is another man's poison.

I'd have to skip a couple of decades ahead before I'd learn more about personality types and how we each express consciousness differently through the prism of our particular mind, heart and psyche. It does seem that, far from being as unique as we'd perhaps imagine, personalities do seem to adhere to certain archetypes and patterns.

At a certain point in my life, I found exploring both the Myer Briggs personality system (MBTI) and the Enneagram of great help. For what it's worth, I conform to the INFJ (the "counsellor") descriptor in the Myer-Briggs system and a Type 9 Enneagram (the "peacemaker"). I found both helpful and the Myer-Briggs descriptor, in particular, provided an surprisingly accurate blueprint of my personality and the way I tend to process reality and relate to the world and others.

Without question, life would have been easier if I'd had access to this knowledge when I was growing up. It might have helped me understand and accept that, in spite of what the motivational speakers might claim, we cannot actually be whoever and whatever we want to be. The simple truth is we are each set up to be a certain way based on an infinite set of configurations beyond our control. Life is not about becoming what we want or what we think the world wants us to be. It's about finding who we were born to be and then having the courage and conviction to *be* that with all our heart and soul.

Whether directly or indirectly, our culture promotes a universal ideal to which we all try to conform. When we fail to do that, the mind tends to turn on itself. We become racked with a sense of failure, inadequacy and shame. This seems to be an almost universal suffering in our modern age. We're each trying to measure up to some elusive and unattainable standard of perfection while savagely berating ourselves for failing to do so.

Certainly, it's a good idea to capitalise on our strengths and minimise our weaker aspects, but we won't get far until we accept our own basic nature; which is called our *swabhava* in Sanskrit. We are each born to be a certain way. The only way to truly succeed and be happy in life is to honour that; to honour our own nature and *be true to who we are.*

According to the Myer-Briggs system, my personality type is the rarest of all. That might go some way to explaining why I felt like an outsider and misfit even at a young age. As it turns out, this sense of "not fitting in" is common to many, if not most, spiritually sensitive people. It's as though we were born with an openness and sensitivity often at odds with other people and our environment. I think this can be particularly hard for boys, because, certainly when I was growing up, there was a pervasive expectation that boys had to be tough and they should never show emotion or sensitivity. Such toxic masculinity can be damaging to children, especially when they simply don't fit the mould.

As a child, I was incredibly open in that I could sense and

read not only people but places and energy. The emotions of others tended to affect me more than they generally should. I found situations of conflict almost unbearable. By some intuitive sense, I could instinctively sense a "good person" from a "bad person" or, rather, the people that were safe to be around from those who were best avoided. I had a softness and depth that was uncommon and I could sense it sometimes made people a little uncomfortable. My grandmother once remarked to my mother that I had a distant, unworldly look in my eyes which somewhat unnerved her. I was intelligent when I applied myself and, by nature, extremely creative. I generally found it more joyful and satisfying drawing and doing any creative work by myself than playing with the other kids.

As school progressed, I grew increasingly aware that I was notably different from others. That sense of alienation was not a nice feeling. By this point, my developing ego had already taken to self-judgement and self-recrimination. I took my softness to be weakness and became self-conscious about my perceived differences from my peers and the fact I tended to be something of a loner. Rather than appreciating and celebrating any differences in myself, I saw it as a sign of inferiority. It didn't help that I often felt strangely transparent, as though I was only ever half there; as though my energy wasn't contained in my body but was scattered halfway across the universe and back.

Moreover, I sometimes, almost unconsciously, felt that I, this "Rory" person, wasn't entirely *real*. Whereas I could perceive that everyone around me had clearly defined boundaries and a strong sense of personality or ego, I seemed to have a less defined self.

Born with a chameleon-like quality, I had the ability to shift my energy and persona to match to my environment and the people around me. This wasn't even something I consciously sought to do. It just so happened I had the inherent tendency to "merge" with the people I was around and adapt myself accordingly. This was something that could, at times, be a good thing while, at other times, depending on who I was around, it was most certainly a dangerous thing.

Whatever the case, it all contributed to a strangely lacking sense of self; the feeling that I wasn't quite a real person; that I was just shifting with the wind and assuming a succession of masks chosen on the basis of whoever and whatever I happened to be around.

Of course, I didn't want anyone to *know* any of this. I'd learned to be guarded around others. It wasn't safe to be too vulnerable and open. You never knew when someone might turn on you and scream at you to "GET OUT OF MY HOUSE!" As a result, although already quite private and even secretive by nature, I became increasingly closed. Years later, my Mum admitted that she had trouble connecting with me during my early years, for I became aloof, self-contained and impenetrable.

I nevertheless possessed a rich inner life. I was gifted with an astonishing imagination and tended to live in my head a great deal. Like most kids, I loved cartoons and comic books, and as much as I consumed, I created. I'd spend hours alone dreaming up entire universes, worlds and stories with full casts of characters in my head. Some of these I would transcribe as my own comic books (and some, many years later, as novels). Most, however, I kept to myself in my own private world of thought and imagination—a world that was often just as real to me as the outer world of the mundane.

I liked my own company, which was just as well, because for quite a few years I didn't have any proper friends. While I wasn't bullied in any sustained fashion, I was, at times, subject to the stunning and incomparable unkindness with which kids often treat each other. That only served to increase the distance I put between myself and others. I could be solitary; but, as I seemed to have worlds within worlds inside of me, that generally didn't bother me. That said, at times I did feel self-conscious or even ashamed about being a loner, for fear that this might signal that there was, indeed, something irredeemably wrong with me.

Once again, if I knew then what I know now, I'd have realised that being an outsider isn't necessarily a bad thing. A persistent theme of this lifetime has been developing the courage to be different, to question the things that hardly anyone else questions, and to tread my own path with as much courage and integrity as I could muster.

That can be hard when we're all hardwired to want to fit in and to gain the approval of others. A large part of my psyche compels me to avoid making waves and yet my *dharma*, my life path, has often necessitated it. Looking back now, I view the child I was with great compassion and understanding. At the time, unfortunately, I learned to become my own biggest and most brutal critic. That seems to be one of the most tragic predicaments of the human race. We may find it easy to love others, and yet, astonishingly, have little else but scorn for ourselves.

The core of this problem is, quite simply, self-judgement. In my case, I felt a certain alienation from my environment and I assumed that I was somehow lacking in some way because I didn't conform to what I thought I "should" be.

A tribal mentality runs deep in all human beings; something instilled in us at a primal level. This manifests as the need to be accepted and validated by the rest of the "tribe". When something happens to threaten that; to make us feel that, in some way, we don't fit in with or match up to others, the damage to the developing psyche can be significant. My instinctive defence mechanism was to close down and retreat deeper into my own world. Little did I know, however, that this closing down may have contributed in some way to my body becoming gravely ill. For by the time I was eight years old, I would suddenly find myself having to fight for my life.

Above: Aged between 5 and 6.

Above: with my parents when we lived in Surrey, England.
Below left: with Mum, my godmother and sister Holly
Below right: on holiday in Cornwall with Holly, ages 6 and 8.

"If a person lives without inner struggle; if everything happens to him without opposition...he will remain such as he is."

G.I. Gurdjieff

Everything Changes

A shaman once told me that when I was eight years old I died and was reborn. That's certainly interesting, because when I was eight I was diagnosed with cancer. Hodgekin's lymphoma, to be precise. I believe it was a rebirth of sorts because it changed everything, not just at the time, but for the rest of my life.

I'd been having symptoms for many months, including fatigue and a strange rash on my face. My GP at the time was less than helpful. I think I was prescribed some antibiotics and, when that didn't help, he basically shrugged his shoulders and said to come back in a few months if nothing had improved.

Fortunately for me, it was around that time that my family moved from Surrey, in England, where I'd spent most my childhood, to the North East of Scotland. My Dad had grown disenchanted with his job as a bank manager and when his parents, my grandparents, decided to retire from running the village shop, Dad agreed to take it over. So, up we moved, and, fortunately, with a change of both house and country, we got a change of doctor.

My symptoms were worsening by that point. My new GP opted to take it seriously. I went into hospital and had all kinds of tests run and that's when they discovered the extent of my illness. I don't remember how I felt upon being told the news. Probably not much. Obviously I'd heard of cancer, but I think I just accepted what I was being told. All I really wanted was simply to get back home—after all, staying in hospital isn't fun at any age, but I was eight and had never even been away from my family at all until then.

Chemotherapy began in earnest. It was no picnic. What I

remember most are the injections—and Dad almost passing out and having to be taken out the room (and not being allowed back in again whenever needles were visible), spending the night vomiting afterward, crippling fatigue and a huge amount of time off school. I was on fortnightly cycles and had tablets to take every day for two weeks, during which time I was too sick to go to school.

It ended up that, for the best part of that year, I was only at school around fifty percent of the time. For a kid, missing school is actually one upside to being ill, but I didn't really like how excluded it made me feel. I was smart and generally did well at school, so I don't think I had much trouble catching up, but I did feel increasingly alienated from the other kids. I don't think I ever really spoke about being ill with my friends and none of them really asked about it. If anything, it was quite an embarrassing thing. I hated the attention and didn't want any fuss. I just got on with things as best I could.

I occasionally found myself getting picked on because of it. There was an announcement put in the school newsletter asking parents of kids in my class to notify the school if their child had any infectious conditions, such as colds or flu, because I was on chemotherapy and my immune system was compromised. I hated the self-consciousness this brought and some of the inevitable questions that came my way. On a couple of occasions, some kids decided to harass me about having cancer. I remember once a group of girls from another year following me home shouting "Cancer reject" at me (I'm still not sure what that even means. These kids may have been among the meanest, but they certainly weren't the brightest). I ignored them, pretending they didn't even exist, and I never told anyone afterward. After all, I tended to cope by holding things in and not expressing how I felt. Such incidents only reinforced that tendency.

My family were amazing and I credit them, Mum especially,

with saving my life. I don't know if I'd still be here had it not been for her ceaseless love and care. I didn't really see the toll that my illness had on her, and my Dad or the rest of my family, because they didn't want me to see that. But it must have been painful and terrifying seeing your child go through such an ordeal and face their mortality at such a young age. Interestingly, many years later, Mum told me that she felt a certain guilt when I was diagnosed because she hadn't felt as close to me as she did with my sister. I don't think I wasn't even aware of that, but it's understandable because I was a somewhat withdrawn, remote, self-contained little kid.

Being critically ill changed everything. I remember Mum would sit holding me at night and, years later, she said that she was trying to heal me at some instinctive level; willing me to get better. At the time, I just felt enveloped by an incredible love and warmth. I'd never felt as safe and loved; for it was like basking in the light of an infinite sun.

Again, it wasn't until years later that we had the discussion, but my illness changed Mum's life in more ways than one. It forced her to turn to God and reignited a spiritual spark within her. She'd always had a strong faith and spirituality and, even from a young age, knew that there was much more to reality than could be perceived with the eyes and senses. Although raised a Christian and having gone to Church her entire life, the strict and dogmatic duality of Christianity didn't provide what she was looking for spiritually.

My illness was the catalyst that set her on another spiritual path; one that forced her to turn inward to find answers and support. She was already unknowingly performing healing on me as she held me and willed me to get better. Over the next few years, she would come to explore her spirituality a lot more, meeting healers, learning meditation and discovering a cornucopia of wisdom from various spiritual traditions. Beautifully, it was out of this time of pain and uncertainty that this spiritual flame grew brighter and it was a light that would pass onto me as I entered my teens.

Nobody in their right mind would invite challenges such as this, but it is often through life's most painful events, the things that shake us to our core, that we are capable of making the greatest spiritual leaps. It's precisely when the world seems to be crumbling around us that we come to find a place deep within ourselves, at the core of our being, where there's perfect calm, peace and stillness; a place where no suffering, sorrow or fear can enter, and where we only know an expansive and all-pervading love and stillness.

Once we find that place, even if only for a glimmer of a second, it changes our lives forevermore. Even if we seem to lose it and immediately get pulled back in the storm, we can never forget that transcendent space of inner serenity and grace, where everything suddenly seems absolutely perfect as it is.

My chemotherapy continued for the best part of a year. The protocol I was on, to my understanding, was a comparatively recent development and increased the odds of survival immensely. Prior to its licensing, the survival rate for what I had was pretty dismal.

My goodness, it knocked the stuffing out of me, though. I kept my hair, which was something. A lot of the other kids I saw at the clinic lost all of their hair. I think I'd have found that pretty tough; not because I was vain at such a tender age, but because it's bad enough to have cancer without looking like you have cancer. I think the main change to my appearance was putting on weight, which was likely down to the steroids. Whereas before I was slender as a rake, I was now succumbing to steroid induced hunger and wasn't exercising much, so I added several pounds and became somewhat stocky. The weight didn't immediately vanish even after treatment, of course, and would later create body image issues when I hit puberty.

At this point, we were living in a house attached to a grocery shop and the shop had several shelves packed with chocolate and all kinds of confectionery. Holly and I used to sneak in when the shop was closed and our parents were otherwise occupied and help ourselves to whatever we fancied. We weren't bad kids by any means, but we had our mischievous side and sometimes the temptation was too great. I mean, we were an eight year old and six year old basically living in a sweet shop—how could we not take advantage of that good fortune?

Aside from chocolate temptation, kids are resilient; often far more so than adults. I never thought of myself as particularly strong. In fact, being the sensitive introvert I was, if anything I thought of myself as weak. But that isn't true, because I managed to weather that storm, and many others, and I did so with grit and resilience, qualities undervalued by many these days.

I don't remember many of the hospital and doctor appointments, for they pretty much blended into each other. But I got to a point where I was, by divine grace, declared as being in remission. It didn't necessarily feel like the greatest victory at the time because I was still feeling unwell from the treatment and would continue to do so for considerable time.

I had checkups every month for a while, and then every three months. With cancer you're never truly out of the woods, although the longer the time passes the safer you generally are. The three month checkups gradually lengthened to every six months. I was told I'd probably be getting them for the rest of my life. That didn't bother me. As far as I was concerned, that part of my life was over and it wasn't something I would lose any sleep over. I'd made it through this trial by fire, and the rest of my life lay ahead of me.

"Have patience. Everything is difficult before it is easy."

Saadi

Being a Teenager
(Is Not as Fun as the Movies Made It Look)

The time between ages nine and twelve was among of the happiest of my life. We had moved, once again, this time to a beautiful seaside town in the North-East of Scotland. Our house was right at the harbour. It was a cool place for a kid to play and the adjacent beach happened to be renowned as one of the loveliest in the entire country. A friend and I used to play at the harbour and go beach combing; trawling the shore for shells and taking note of the various signs of life we came across (yeah, we were geeks, but there are worse things to be!). There were so many great places to walk and play, invariably accompanied by our crazy, boisterous and always exuberant boxer dog, Cleo. I remember it as a carefree, happy, innocent time.

I'd been declared cancer free, although some of the aftereffects of the treatment, particularly the fatigue and lack of vitality, continued and would do so rather indefinitely. That particular storm cloud, however, was no longer hovering above me. My beloved grandparents moved to the next town, barely a stone's throw away, which was an added bonus. I'd always been a creative kid, and I began creating my own comic books and spent many hours happily scribbling away. My school teachers loved reading them and offered a great deal of encouragement. I never had any doubt that my future lay in writing and publishing in some form.

Of course, entropy set in, as it always does, and, when I was thirteen, we moved house again. While it was a nice house in the country surrounded by trees (and whisky distilleries, as it happened), I missed my old home and friends and never entirely felt at home there even though I lived there the best part of a decade. There was a darker energy to the place and, while there were certainly plenty of good times, I don't look back on it with much fondness. By this point, I was in my second year at High School and I'd been fairly happy at my old school. The new one, not so much.

For a teenager, few things are quite as awful as moving to a new school. Everyone has already formed their circles of friends and there's a certain status quo you have to suss in order to find your place. It was tough; I'd made friends at my old school, but forging friendships as the new kid was a challenge—particularly as a natural introvert who felt more comfortable blending in with the scenery than pushing myself forward. I guess fear of rejection was an underlying motivator, too. The moment you hit your teen years, you tend to become hyperconscious of just about everything; not least yourself and how you might be perceived by others.

I don't suppose anyone's teenage years are a smooth ride. Those seven years between ages thirteen and twenty are unquestionably ones of profound transformation, not just physically, but psychologically, emotionally and even societally, as we move from the carefree abandon of childhood to trying to figure out our place in the world and set a future trajectory for ourselves.

Looking back now, I see the axis of my teen years as a struggle between who I wanted to be, who I thought the world wanted me to be, and who I actually was. These three aspects often seemed at loggerheads. Yet while I found myself struggling with matters of personal identity, along with feelings of alienation and loneliness, this was also the time when a spiritual spark ignited in my heart and I started down a path that would eventually, in the fullness of time, lead to liberation. But, boy, it wouldn't be an easy road getting to that point.

The first year or so at my new school was a particular struggle. I dreaded getting up in the morning. While I got on fine with my classmates, for the longest time I felt like an outsider and it took what seemed like an eternity before I made any actual friends. When they already have their established friend groups and cliques, school kids don't have much impetus to take pity on the newbie.

At lunch time, rather than sit alone in the crowded canteen and common areas with their echoing cacophony of noise, I would leave the school grounds and go walk by myself; anywhere really—along the housing estates, past the shops, down various streets and parks—just to pass the time and get some space and quiet. On days which Mum was off work I'd beg her to take me home for lunch (we lived miles out of town, so it wasn't exactly within walking distance). Not to sound self-pitying, but I must have seemed like that enigmatic, strange kid; one of those "weirdo" loners who stuck out like a sore thumb. Heck, if it had been a decade later I could have just worn black, grown my hair, painted my nails and called myself an "emo" (hey, I guess if you're feeling miserable, you might as well make an art out of it).

On the bright side, I liked my own company and, beyond a certain point, I'd never been all that sociable anyway. Oh, I enjoyed being with others to a point, but after that point I found myself drained and depleted and needed time alone to recover. Part of me felt comfortable being that way because it was just the way I naturally seemed to be. But another, pained part of myself, felt ashamed, alone and inferior.

Looking back, I feel a sense of compassion for the boy that I was. Here I was, this painfully sensitive yet outwardly aloof kid, sweet by nature, kind and fairly pure by worldly standards, idealistic, creative and uncommonly spiritual for my age. Some of these qualities were noticed and encouraged by teachers, but they had little market value in the jungle of High School.

After all, any hint of difference in the schoolyard is tantamount to a bullseye on your back. At times, I did find myself a target. I could never figure why some kids had to be so cruel and, of course, the bullies always managed to sniff out even the slightest hint of difference or vulnerability in others. I did often find myself in the line of fire until I came to a point where I learned to fortify my defences and project an air of "don't mess with me". Interestingly, the moment I learned to change my energy and cover up any sign of vulnerability, others treated me differently. So, I learned at quite an early age that the way others treat us tends to mirror the way we feel about ourselves.

I have to admit that by this time, the world in which I found myself, and the world in general, often felt like a dark and unwelcoming place. I found the prevalent culture crude and empty. One of the girls in my year once said that her one word description of me was "innocent" and, sure enough, I'd certainly started with a certain innocence and naivety about me.

My ideals were at odds with the modern culture and the more that I learned about the world, the more I just didn't understand it. Virtually all my peers seemed to simply accept the status quo, whereas I questioned everything, at least inwardly. I didn't understand why human beings had to be so hateful and violent to each other, to animals and to the planet. I couldn't understand why people had to make life such a hell for themselves and others. Whereas when I was younger, the world seemed a magical place in many respects, the more I learned about life, the more I found certain aspects of the world and the human condition horrifying.

By that point, I was beginning to feel like some awkward hybrid of naive, geeky kid and world weary philosopher.

Meanwhile, most of my schoolmates began fixating on the two holy grails of adolescence: alcohol and sex.

As we all know, the onslaught of the teenage years never comes alone. It's accompanied by a deluge of hormones and ever shifting moods and emotions. In no time at all, everything seems to change: not only our bodies, but our personality, likes and dislikes, values and needs and our very identity.

We're also liable to begin learning things about ourselves that we'd never imagined or perhaps never wanted to imagine. In my case, that included fact I was gay, although it took me a long time to actually admit it to myself. While society has changed considerably over the past twenty-five years and same sex attraction is generally no longer seen as a big thing (although for people in many parts of the world it sadly still is), back in the Nineties it was a huge, earth-shattering thing, particularly for a teenager. I didn't know a single person who was openly non-heterosexual, at least to my knowledge, and the only representation on television and film happened to be stereotypically effeminate comic relief characters and maybe the odd camp psychotic villain.

Whereas it now almost seems trendy among younger people to be gender non-conforming or some subset of the LGBTQ alphabet soup, when I was growing up it would have amounted to social suicide. If anyone had come out as anything other than straight when I was at school their lives would have been made a living hell; a beaten up, bricks through the window and family potentially disowning you kind of hell. I guess it was impossible not to internalise a degree of homophobia when, from a young age, the very worst insult you could be called in the playground was "gay" or its various derogatory derivatives. I still have no idea why. It's without doubt a stupid thing to get worked up about. We have no control over who we happen to be attracted to and love is love, so what does it even matter? Of course, it shouldn't.

The very thought, however, that I might be anything other than "normal" was too terrifying to consider. It just wasn't safe to go there, so I bricked that up behind a fortified wall. It's something I wouldn't deal with until I was in my early twenties and realised that you have to face your issues rather than hide from them. Until then, although the thought I wasn't quite "right" chewed away at my self-esteem, I did my best just to be like everyone else.

Again, my natural survival instinct was to withdraw and retreat. Putting up walls around myself and keeping a distance between myself and others seemed to be a reflex response that kept me in a certain comfort zone. It came with a price, of course: the pain of isolation, feeling different and not part of the tribe. If there's one thing a teenager wants to avoid at all costs, it's the horror of feeling different to others. But what are you going to do when you clearly *are* different? Although some people evidently get an ego-kick by emphasising just how "special" and "unique" they are, it was quite the opposite for me.

On the bright side, the challenges that come our way always come with opportunities for growth, resilience and healing. I learned certain skills for navigating my environment; skills that put me in good stead throughout the rest of my life. As an outsider, I was very much an observer of people. I learned that looking from the outside-in grants a perspective and insight that others generally lack. You really see how people tick, especially if you have an empathic streak, which I most definitely did. That really helps build relationships because people love nothing more than to feel understood. Funnily enough, I often understood people more than they seemed to understand themselves and, on that basis, I learned to connect and communicate with people.

In true chameleon fashion, I had the ability adapt myself to my surroundings and to at least appear that I was blending in and that I belonged. Learning to push past my innate shyness and mask my self-esteem issues, I eventually found it easier to make friends.

My first group of friends at my new school were, in retrospect, not the best match for me. Passive aggressive at best, they made an art out of ridiculing everyone and everything. I suppose I was welcomed into the group because I could be pretty funny and goofy and I obviously was amusing enough to hang out with. I didn't really belong, however, and I never opened myself up to any of them. Which is just as well, because anything that was remotely alien to the group dynamic was immediately shot down with ridicule.

The head of this particular peer group was an especially cynical guy adept at negating the worth of others in order to bolster his own. I didn't even realise what was happening at the time, but in retrospect I can see how, ironically, I was bullied by my own supposed friends. There can be a fine line between the usual teen banter and the death of a thousand cuts, in which you find yourself repeatedly shot down and ridiculed in both subtle and overt ways for pretty much anything and everything, including, at times, just opening my mouth to speak. It was not a healthy dynamic and it's only looking back now that I can see the terrible effect it had in terms of my sense of insecurity and worthlessness. Why I let it happen for so long I don't know, other than perhaps I didn't see or care to admit what was actually going on.

Through a process of adaptation and assimilation, we tend to become like the people we spend our time with. That's why we must always be discriminating about who we let into our sphere of influence. I knew these guys could, like all teenagers, be assholes and when I was around them I could be an asshole too. I'd go along with things and say and do things that didn't sit right with me just in order to fit in; all so I could pass myself off as being one of the gang. There's a real pain involved in not living in alignment with who you are and I felt it most acutely in my teen years.

What I did, however, was keep my boundaries. I rarely hung around with them much outside of school, which eventually set some noses out of joint. Besides finding socialising exhausting and still suffering ongoing health issues, mainly in the form of persistent fatigue, I cherished my own time to rest and recharge, to have my own space and to relax free of the persona I had to adopt for other people. Plus, I loved time with my family, even as I became an increasingly sullen teenager.

The curse of the introvert is an internal dichotomy; a seesaw between wanting to be alone and simultaneously craving connection with others. Internal dualities and contradictory inner impulses can be a real pickle, but what can you do? After a time, I pretty much burned my bridges with my group of so-called friends. They knew I wasn't really part of the group and I knew it too, so that was no great loss. Not content with beer and alcopops, they ended up getting into hard drugs and that was an avenue I had no intention of going down.

Miserable although that period of time had been, by my final year in school, things changed. I experienced a subtle but profound inner transformation; one that was to mark the beginning of my spiritual journey.

Part 1: Becoming A Person

19 years old in Majorca, Spain

"Even when tied in a thousand knots, the string is still but one."

Rumi

Thank Goodness It's Not Just Me

If you've read this far, I commend you. I've tried to keep details to a minimum to avoid boring people with irrelevant personal minutiae. In writing this, one of the things I wanted to illustrate was how, as we grow up, we develop a deep rooted problem, or, indeed, set of problems, centred around our sense of self, or the person we think we are.

Don't believe me? Then try to think of a single problem that doesn't somehow, in some way, relate to "self"; whether self in relation to self and others, or self in relation to past or future events.

This small-self isn't something we're born with, but rather something that develops in tandem with our bodies and minds. When a baby arrives in the world, it doesn't have to do anything at all in order to warrant being loved and adored by its parents. In time, however, as our ego and the sense of being a differentiated, autonomous "self" begin developing, so, too, do all the various concepts and ideas we build around it, not least the notion of whether that self, "our self", is either a good or bad one. If we're lucky, our immediate family continue to see us as a faultless delight, but, in time, it begins dawning on us that the love, approval and validation of others is far from unconditional.

Whereas, once upon a time, every single drawing we scrawled was treated like a Picasso by our mother, when we end up at school suddenly everything we do isn't so perfect. Indeed, we find we have to pass tests, exams and assessments in order to gain approval. Then, of course, come the school report cards passing summary judgement of our merit or lack thereof. Although I was pretty good at most of my school subjects, my behaviour wasn't always impeccable, largely a result of the company I was keeping, and there were times when I could practically see the storm clouds gather at home when I was handed a report card. I remember on one occasion taking a pen and trying to forge the teacher's handwriting in order to add a comment or two that didn't sound quite so damning (spoiler: my hasty amendments didn't look as convincing as I'd hoped).

We all want and crave approval. When we don't receive it, it can cut deep, because we take it as an affront to our very self, our very being. Of course, that's to say nothing of the approval and validation we crave from our peers, based as it is on a whole other set of fickle and sometimes unfathomable criteria. Needless to say, as the years pass, we assemble the sense of being a particular type of person; a person with both good and bad qualities, with various strengths and weaknesses, successes and failings.

Although always a mixture of the two, a duality of positive and negative—the mind mercilessly accentuates the bad. In general, we tend to focus on our perceived failings and shortcomings instead of appreciating and cherishing our strengths and skills. The mind, essentially a survival tool, naturally zeroes in on the negative; on perceived threats and lack. That was its way of keeping us safe and alive in precarious, danger filled environments such as prehistoric jungles and plains populated by hungry lions and tigers. Unfortunately, this primal survival mechanism functions to this very day and generates a whole lot of mind-made suffering for we poor humans.

At the time, I thought it was just me. But virtually all of us grow up with a distorted view of ourselves in which we fixate on all the things we perceive as flawed, lacking or weak.

How is it possible to love ourselves, to accept ourselves and be truly happy when, at our very core, we have this gaping chasm of self-condemnation, insufficiency and lack—something that tends to be constantly reinforced by both the media and culture we live in?

While everybody has their own list of reasons why they aren't quite good enough, the fundamental wound is the same in all human beings.

It's painful to feel limited and lacking. This pain compels us to do all kinds of not so healthy things; not least ceaselessly chasing eternal happiness in the world of ephemeral objects. We think that if we could just be thinner, or more muscular, or more popular, or have a boyfriend or girlfriend, a husband or a wife, a child, a business, or a Nobel Peace Prize, we'll finally feel happy and satisfied with who we are. But unless we deal with the underlying cause, the solutions will be little more than bandaids.

I wish I'd known all this when I was a teenager. One of the greatest mistakes I made was comparing how I felt inwardly with how others presented themselves outwardly. If only I'd known that I wasn't the only who felt like this; that everyone else, despite their outward bravado and swagger, also struggled at some level with this sense of incompleteness and fear of not being enough.

It's not personal. It just felt that way when I was growing up. I felt like a mistake; that I'd been manufactured defectively and that I didn't belong in the world around me. This is nothing to do with the way I was raised, because I was loved and cared for exceptionally well and, unlike a great many on the planet, had material stability and security. It seems that wasn't enough to insulate me from what I internalised from my environment, from others and even from the influence of media. I imagine the latter is a much greater issue for teenagers these days thanks to the ubiquitous nature of social media and the internet. I can only say I'm glad that social media wasn't around when I was growing up.

Here's the thing, though. Here's where my story began to change. I was around sixteen years old when I discovered a secret that set me on a different path; one that would change the course of my life forevermore.

This sense of self that was causing so many problems for me? I was about to discover that it wasn't who I *really* was. It was just a program, and programs can be changed.

"A single moment of understanding can flood a whole life with meaning."

Anon

A Greater Reality

My generation was the first to be raised under the paradigm of what we call Neoliberalism (not to be confused with regular liberalism; two quite different things).

Neoliberalism, shepherded in the 80's by Margaret Thatcher and then Ronald Reagan in the USA, is an economic doctrine emphasising competition within a free market. More than that, it is also an ideology at the root of much government policy and, more crucially, the way we are trained to view ourselves, others and the environment around us. Neoliberalism conditions us to see ourselves as a brand; as a perfectible product existing in a dog-eat-dog world. Whether we succeed or fail at any endeavour is seen as strictly up to *us* rather than any environmental or deterministic factors—and any failure, is first and foremost, a failure of our own self.

Back to this notion of self, again. My teenage years weren't much fun, not so much because of what was going on, but because of how ruthlessly self critical I'd become. As the notion of self and identity becomes the unconscious pinnacle of our existence, our psyche is constantly on guard, desperate to both protect and enhance our sense of self. As I didn't feel a fit for the world around me—being, as I was, an introvert in an extrovert's world, hiding from my sexual orientation out of fear of rejection and having completely different values to most the people around me—I took that as a failing in myself.

I felt flawed and defective, and the more I felt that way, they more I withdrew from others. I didn't let people get close to me because I was convinced if they saw the real me they would reject or ridicule me. Nobody wants to be a misfit and no one really wants to feel different and "other than" at that tender age.

We crave to fit in because we are driven, at an almost primal level, to seek the validation and approval of others—not for its own sake, either, but so we can then validate and approve of ourselves.

By the time I was fourteen or fifteen, I wasn't at all comfortable in my own skin. I felt alone and alienated even when I was with people at school because I was just aware that I was so different. I couldn't let people see the "real me", so I put up a front. I developed body image issues and, determined to at least be in control of something, decided to lose weight by not eating during the day. It worked, and I kept the weight off, too, but it wasn't a healthy way to effect change, being motivated more out of despair than self care.

One day, however, I caught sight of a book in my mother had been reading. Ever since my battle with cancer several years beforehand, Mum had been set upon a spiritual path which took her outside of conventional religion and brought her to alternative spiritual material, including self-help books and topics such as meditation and healing. The book that caught my eye was by Louise L Hay, a highly influential teacher whose most famous work was "You Can Heal Your Life". I can't remember the name of this particular book, but something drew me to it and, rather than ask Mum if I could borrow it, which I found strangely embarrassing, I snuck the book out of her room and read as much as I could before returning it.

What I read was exactly what I needed at that time in my life. It immediately helped change my perception of myself and the world around me. It shifted my thinking and suddenly gave me a whole lot of hope and a greater sense of empowerment.

I can't entirely remember my takeaways from that Louise Hay book, but it got me on the path to realising that this self I was taking to be "me" was not, in actual fact, who I really was.

Given all the problems I was having with it, that was, of course, a blessed relief!

Indeed, the person I assumed I was was nothing but an assorted bundle of thoughts, programming and conditioning. Not only that, but it was something malleable; something that could be changed. Hay was very much into affirmations: short, positive statements designed to reprogram the mind. Admittedly, some of her prescribed affirmations sounded a little naff, but I started experimenting with the ones that resonated.

Sure enough, in the days and weeks that followed, I began noticing a difference. I began taking it easy on myself and beating myself up less. I began to relax all this tension I had about the person I thought I was versus the person I thought the world wanted me to be. Little by little, I began realising that it was okay to be different from others; to see things in a contrasting way and to hold my own values and priorities.

As I continued reading, exploring and experimenting in this manner, I began to realise what I'd always intuitively known in my heart of hearts: that there was much more to reality than could ever be comprehended with the mind and senses alone.

The world and this person I appeared to be, were, in fact, just tiny things compared to the vast, unseen dimension—*of what? Spaciousness? Light? Energy?*—I could somehow feel and intuit all around and within me.

This spiritual spark continued growing, and I felt as though I was coming home to myself. At school and with friends I was still the same old Rory and I engaged with others as I was expected to. I still joined in the same bullshit conversations about complete nonsense while inwardly knowing that I was just playing a role; that it wasn't really "me", and that was okay.

I began feeling with the entirety of my being that I was here in this world for some kind of purpose, some deeper reason, and that my path may be different than the one trodden by most others. This gave me an enormous boost; knowing that there was some meaning to my existence, even if no one else was capable of understanding it but me. I knew it somehow tied into creativity and sharing some kind of message with the world. What the message was, I wasn't entirely sure, but I was certain it had to do with the realisation that there was a greater Reality and a deeper meaning to life; that the level of form was but the tip of some vast, cosmic iceberg.

It's probably no coincidence that this was around the time my creativity began to flourish. I'd always been a creative child, and I spent most of my free time drawing comic books and dreaming up my own stories, characters, worlds and adventures. Now there was something deeper behind my work. I felt I actually had something to say, even though I wasn't yet sure quite what or how to convey it.

I do know that I was only sixteen when I began working on a novel that would take many years to refine and eventually publish. It was originally titled "The Journey" and I initially envisaged as a film or series of films. It would be over a decade before I'd actually manage to complete it to my satisfaction: as a novel; the first in a planned series. Retitled "The Key of Alanar", it was a project immensely close to my heart and one I utterly poured my heart and soul into. It was eventually published in 2015 and re-published in 2017. Unfortunately, it bombed commercially—and I mean absolutely bombed. I've still no idea why because it remains the work of which I'm most proud. It may have been my greatest failure on one level, but to me, artistically and creatively, it probably remains my greatest triumph.

But I'm getting ahead of myself here. Where was I? Still back in high school, nearing my final year. Ironically, it wasn't until my final year that I actually halfway began enjoying school.

Perhaps it was because I'd gotten all the qualifications I thought I needed during my penultimate year—and excellent grades, too—so I relaxed and pretty much coasted for that final year.

I felt buoyed by my secret new spiritual life and, by the time I was seventeen, I was reading as many spiritual books as I could, meditating regularly and was somehow able to "tap into" this greater Reality that I knew interfaced and pervaded the outer world of appearances and forms.

Knowing I was a part of that spiritual Reality seemed to make life at times almost effortlessly easy; there was much greater flow and peace. I stepped away from the people that I knew were not good for me to be around. I learned that, in spite of being an introvert, I was nevertheless able to make friends and connect with people and that gave me greater social confidence. I was learning that the appearance of separation was actually just an illusion and all people, all beings, were somehow connected and one at an intrinsic, fundamental level. That knowledge really did change things for me. There was, however, a long way to go.

"Do not seek outside yourself. For it will fail, and you will weep each time an idol fails."

A Course in Miracles

The Pendulum Swings

Looking back over this lifetime, I can see a relentless seesaw between the way I wanted my life to be and the way that God, the Universe, or Fate (call it what you will) wanted it to be. Me (or rather, my ego) versus God? Obviously that was an argument I was never going to win. But that didn't stop me from trying—and I tried so very hard, for years, to impose my own will and to create the life I thought I wanted.

When I left school I got a place at a prestigious art school. It seemed the obvious next step in my life as I'd gravitated to art from a young age. Alas, my time at art school was short and highlighted the pendulum swing my life would take for the next decade. Every time I took a step into the wider world, filled with ambition and the desire to succeed, you could guarantee that inevitably, in the weeks, months or perhaps years to follow, it would be followed by a swift backward step; a swerve that kept me from fully losing myself in worldly life and which always brought me back to a lonesome inward focus.

But, oh boy, it would be considerable time before I finally heeded the message. It would have saved a great deal of unnecessary suffering if only I'd grasped this particular lesson sooner and surrendered to the way things wanted to be. One of the downsides of so much modern spirituality is the delusion that the key to success in life is attempting to use God to get what we want. That might sound irresistible to the ego, and it certainly sells books, courses and seminars, but the real secret to life is coming into alignment with what God wants for us.

Starting university necessitated a move to the bright lights, noise and bustle of the big city. Talk about a shock to the system. The days were surprisingly long and exhausting; I didn't particularly feel settled at the art school and I lacked confidence in my abilities. Rather than risk doing something imperfectly and feeling like a complete failure, I tended not to do anything at all and thus my struggle with perfectionism (or, more accurately, perfection paralysis) began. While I understand the necessity of critique and evaluation when it comes to learning, I found the joy of creating stripped away when everything I did was then graded out of a hundred with apparent mathematical precision.

There was a lot of socialising, too; late nights, early mornings, and truckloads of alcohol. While I still had that spiritual fire glowing inside my heart, it was generally set aside and subsumed by another, then-stronger impulse: the desire to both be like others and to be liked by others. I suppose I just wanted just to be a regular teenager, and to fit in and hedonistically enjoy life in a way I hadn't at high school. To my astonishment, I succeeded.

None of that, however, brought the happiness I thought it would. Instead, I felt like even more of an imposter, for I could never shake the feeling that I wasn't being true to myself. I needn't have worried. Life was about to stage an intervention anyway.

Three months after starting art school, I came down with a severe bout of glandular fever which also infected my liver. My health had been a long-term struggle as it was and this illness left me with what was later diagnosed as Myalgic Encephalomyelitis/M.E. or Chronic Fatigue Syndrome, which I think I'd actually already had to a greater or lesser degree since my recovery from cancer ten years before.

I hated this diagnosis almost as much as the condition. Largely due to the fact that doctors had little to no understanding of its cause, a great deal of ignorance and prejudice surrounded it. I was damn near embarrassed to share the diagnosis with anyone lest I receive the frequent and dismissive response, "Oh, I always feel tired, too." There was no equivalence, however, between someone working a full-time job and partying at the weekends with the predicament I now found myself in. It was a struggle simply to get out of bed and do even the smallest of daily tasks without ending up exhausted and in pain.

Given that post viral fatigue was not uncommon after viral infections, I fervently prayed it would pass. It didn't. Instead, it lingered and, although it could be variable—for there were times when it wasn't as bad and I could function a bit more normally as well as times when it exacerbated and flared up horrendously—it had a hugely restricting affect upon my life. With only a fraction of the strength I'd had just months ago, I was unable to return to art school, and my entire life contracted overnight and remained that way for three and a half years.

I was, however, precisely where I was meant to be, although I perhaps wouldn't recognise that for years to come. Hindsight is a wonderful thing, of course. One of the perversities of life is that things seldom make much sense until we're able to look back and finally see how the individual threads come together to create the tapestry of our lives.

"Give me the beauty of the inward soul: may the outward and the inward man be at one."

Socrates

Dance of Duality

For the next few years, I did everything that I could to regain my health. I learned that conventional medicine may be unparalleled at dealing with acute conditions, but is altogether less adept at treating chronic conditions. So, as well as seeing a consultant microbiologist, I relied upon diet, rest, exercise and various healing modalities, of which Qi Gong, or Zhan Zhuang (a form of standing exercise) prove the most effective.

My spirituality also blossomed at this point. I was becoming adept at meditation, joined a meditation group, I learned Reiki and other healing methods courtesy of a nearby spiritual teacher and developed an incredible love of nature and animals. In spite of the challenges I faced, I was using the time to come into myself more; to learn, to grow and to expand more into who and what I truly was. The only spiritual literature I had at the time tended to be New Age and, thus, combined elements of truth and untruth, but it was enough to sustain me at this early stage.

I returned to a local college to study art on a part time basis, and then, as my health generally improved for a few years, changed to a degree in Social Science, which included topics as vast as sociology, psychology, politics, history and philosophy.

By this point, I was twenty-two years old and my health had stabilised, at least for a time. I was able to study full time and even work part time as well in my final year. I was a good student; the top of my class, in fact, and I somehow managed to juggle that with a social life and a group of friends I genuinely adored and who adored me.

I never lost my determination to be a writer; and, although progress was slow and rife with trial and error, I worked as hard as I could on my first novel. I burned myself out with regularity, for my health continued to be precarious, even as I embraced the college party lifestyle. It so happened that, despite my introvert nature, I could also be the life and soul of the party—and, although probably not the wisest of life skills, I could drink just about anyone under the table.

A person's twenties are often geared to consolidating a more cohesive ego identity; one that becomes ever more deeply rooted; an infrastructure likely to remain in place for the remainder of a lifetime. My early twenties were no different. In spite of the spiritual progress I'd seemingly made, I was also driven by an unconscious attempt to build a stronger and more cohesive sense of ego-self, fuelled by the desire to connect with others and to make something of my life and self. As a teenager, I'd felt isolated and disconnected from others, no doubt in part due to the walls I built around myself. The effects of that lingered. Still constrained by a low self-esteem and, driven by the need to compensate for that, when the opportunity arose, my focus turned to the outer world. On one level, I was tired of feeling isolated and different; like some kind of ghost in the world. I decided I wanted to enjoy life as most others my age were.

With increased health, I pushed myself past my old comfort zone, found greater connection and realised that, lo and behold, I was actually considered popular, well liked and attractive by others.

I felt stronger and better able to deal with certain issues I'd been burying for years. That included acknowledging my sexuality. It's something which, I realised, is not self-chosen but pre-configured in the factory settings. I'd learned the necessity of self-acceptance and making peace with the person I was. The only alternative was suffering and I'd already been there, done that. Resistance of any kind, I'd learned, was a recipe for pain. It was daunting telling family and friends something I'd hidden away at the back of my psyche for years. But I quickly realised that the people who truly love us generally do so for who we are at heart, and not because of incidental characteristics and attributes.

I learned a lot about integrity, honesty and having the courage to be true to my nature as a person. I had to accept that, no matter how hard we try in life, there will always be someone ready to hate and find fault with us. What can we do about that? I'd always been exceptionally sensitive to others, but over the years learned to develop a thicker skin and not allow other peoples' bullshit to knock me too far off centre. I also knew that, while some people tend to lose themselves in labels and identity politics, I never wanted myself to be defined by my sexual orientation any more than I wanted to be defined by having blue eyes. Of course, I instinctively knew that there was a vastness to my true nature, to what I really was, and all the constituent parts of my personality and psyche were but incidental components.

Over these years, the seesaw continued between a desire to embrace worldly life and a strong inward pull to this ever present spiritual flame in my heart. That flame never extinguished, even when my attention was, for a few years in my early twenties, consistently redirected to my studies, social life and a number of rocky relationships with generally incompatible guys.

I certainly learned a lot about myself as a person and the problems of samsara, or worldly suffering, which comes from seeking happiness and completeness in the impermanent and insubstantial. Most people grudgingly accept this state of affairs either because they don't realise any alternative could possibly exist or because, in spite of the suffering and sorrows of life in duality, they manage to squeeze out just enough pleasure and satisfaction to compensate for the many bumps and bruises.

That's what I did for a few years. My newfound confidence, however, remained tenuous. Deep inside, I felt unsure of myself as I vacillated between my new larger than life (yet still false) persona and the deeper spiritual knowledge that I was ultimately none of this; but something beyond all form, identity and limitation. Was I *really* being true to who and what I was? I'd come to feel like a walking set of contradictions; presenting a front to the world while inwardly knowing that it was all a big lie.

I needn't have worried. Life always had a way of course correcting for me, even if it often happened in painful ways. It was time to finally and truly *get real*.

I genuinely can't remember where the pirate hat came from.

"Happiness is your nature. It is not wrong to seek it. What is wrong is seeking it outside when it is inside."

Ramana Maharshi

Unwitting Sannyasi

By the time I was twenty-nine, life had gotten tougher; specifically, my health. While I'd had a few years of being at least semi-functional in the world, a virulent bout of flu left me suffering the aftereffects of chronic fatigue with greater severity than ever. There would be no quick fixes this time. Again, my world contracted more or less overnight. I had no choice but to quit my job and spend much of my time resting, for even minor exertions had the potential to floor me, leaving me ill for days or weeks.

As before, the doctors could offer little help, other than trying neurological drugs; the only effect of which tended to be the unwanted side effects. I tried so many things to get better, from outrageously priced alternative therapies to private consultations and extensive blood testing; the latter of which showed impaired mitochondrial function, although both the cause and solution seemed elusive. I began coughing up blood and having strange pains, but, again, when the initial tests showed nothing the doctors tended to shrug their shoulder. I'd give up, too exhausted and discouraged to keep pushing for more tests from an already overburdened health service.

This was also a time in which a number of relationships dissipated. I lost my grandparents within a couple of years of each other. That was an enormous blow, for I'd been closer to them than a lot of people are to their own parents.

Most of my core friends began relocating to other parts of the country or world. I'd also been in a relationship for five years, and that gradually imploded. Over time, I'd come to realise that the two of us simply didn't share the same values and barely any shared interests. We simply didn't speak the same language and

I could no longer pretend to be like "others" for the sake of fitting in; I simply had no energy to maintain such a pretence. It felt like we'd degenerated into an old married couple with virtually nothing left to say each other so we just sat and watched junk on the television. I wanted more than that; more from a relationship and more from life. Quite what exactly, I wasn't sure.

Not out of choice, I became a solitary creature again. The fates had decided that I needed to be what in India is called a *sannyasi*, or renunciate; someone with no worldly ties who can devote their entire life to enlightenment through Self-Realisation. Looking back now, I see what a blessing and a golden opportunity that was. I wasn't always a willing sannyasi, however. There were times when I was; when I knew with certainty that I was on the right path, doing what most mattered to me. At other times, I steadfastly resisted the new state of affairs. Being a sometimes obstinate and stubborn individual, it wasn't something that I would have chosen, even if it was ultimately what I needed.

My family were of enormous support, particularly my Mum; a kindred spirit and someone with whom my values and spiritual outlook closely aligned. Even when life took some tougher turns, I still felt blessed, supported and conscious of just how much I had to be grateful for.

That isn't to say I didn't experience a lot of emotional pain. I got hit pretty hard by the samsara stick, even if it wasn't always outwardly apparent. I not only had to deal with diminished physical health, but I happened to be conscious that time was marching on and that I still hadn't found my place in life. Despite my determination and perfectionism, everything that I set my hand to seemed to fail; disappearing like pebbles sinking to the bottom of a pond while leaving barely a ripple. I'd long known that I was here to contribute something to the world; to give of myself somehow, but the all important matters of *what* and *how* had yet to reveal themselves. Instead, for a number of years I felt utterly stuck and uncertain how to move forward.

Modern culture conditions us to believe that we need to justify our existence. Rather than seeing our worth and value as something innate and inalienable, we superimpose it upon external factors; upon what we do, what we have and our achievements and attainments. At times, I felt rather ashamed of my lack of worldly success. I imagined that anyone looking from the outside would only have seen some loser whose health was compromised by an invisible condition that doctors were at a loss to deal with; and who outwardly looked fine but couldn't make it through the day without returning to bed every few hours. Whereas others my age were generally now married with families and mortgages, I had nothing but myself, my spiritual fixation, and a dream of being a writer. Perhaps, once upon a time, there was something romantic about a penniless writer struggling to get by; but it sure as hell didn't feel romantic to me.

What could I do, though? Much of my money was spent on trying to get better, with little tangible result. I was far from lazy and pushed myself even when I was physically exhausted; forcing myself to write and to get better and more skilled at it, knowing that I had books I felt I had to write and share with the world.

I had to push through an incredible amount of self doubt and insecurity along the way; relating to my worth as a person, the value of my work and even my body itself. My mind tended to project a lot of my insecurity onto my physical body and looks; perhaps because it was something tangible that I could try to control. I'd had body image issues since I was a teen, and that seemed to amplify as my life contracted. I was often told I was good-looking and handsome but what I saw when I looked in the mirror wasn't necessarily what others saw. It's perhaps no surprise that as I fixated on my perceived flaws, my self-esteem plummeted.

Of course, in time, I realised that the only real problem happened to be faulty patterns of thought. My mind, being the problem solving mechanism that it is, was desperately trying to control anything that it could, even if its efforts were distorted and misdirected. Fortunately, I began to see these unhealthy thought patterns for what they were. I then worked exceptionally hard to eradicate them and to redirect my mind to thoughts of truth.

I hesitated to share much of the above. I didn't want to bombard the reader with what might seem like endless and irrelevant personal ramblings. I decided to keep it in, however, to illustrate an important point; one that I don't think can be underemphasised.

Whether we're aware of it or not, the basic human problem is almost always rooted in a diminished sense of "self"; the poisonous notion that who and what we are as a person isn't quite enough.

Tragically, most people waste their time trying to fix the surface level manifestations of the issue without ever getting to the actual root of the problem. It's impossible to escape samsara so long as everything you're doing is actually reinforcing it. Until we confront and resolve this idea of a diminished self and see it for the lie that it is, we can never truly experience wholeness and freedom.

I was learning this bit by bit, and, by God's grace, I would get there in time.

For the next few years, aside from trying to get my health back onto an upward trajectory, I had little else to do but focus upon the few things I could do; namely, writing, getting my mind into gear and, of course, my ever growing commitment to pursuing enlightenment. I knew enough to realise that the only solution to the varied and endless problems of "self" lay in the knowledge that this wasn't our true Self at all.

But how did this intellectual understanding equate to freedom? I kept reading and listening to a cornucopia of spiritual materials, most of which made perfect sense to me. Even though things had yet to "click", I remained convinced that enlightenment existed. I knew there *must* be a solution to life's dichotomy of pleasure and pain; something greater, something truer, more real and lasting.

It was a lofty undertaking without doubt, but I knew that it was possible to crack the code and find a way to end the suffering endemic to the human condition. Even if I was at times an unwilling sannyasi, I was, nevertheless, *in*, and my search for spiritual liberation intensified. I simply knew there was more to life, and more to my own Self, and I was committed to finding it. I had to. It was all that I had left.

Part 2

THE FLAME IGNITES

"The real voyage of discovery consists not of seeking new lands, but in seeing with new eyes."

Marcel Proust

More to Life

Life never made much sense to me without spirituality factored into the equation. That was my way of making sense of not just reality—but, indeed, myself.

While I have the greatest respect for science, I feel it's important to emphasise that the material sciences pertain only to the material world. They offer nothing when it comes to the ultimate cause, meaning and purpose of life. In other words, science will never touch God, because it simply isn't equipped to do that. A means of knowledge is specific to that knowledge. Just as you'll never be able to determine the colour of an object using your nose or ears, the answers to the deepest questions of life—the so-called "unanswerables"—will forever be outside the purview of the physical sciences.

From the time I was just a child, I had the overwhelming conviction that there was more to reality than could be perceived by the senses alone; and so much more to each of us.

Certainly, it so happens that our physical senses are tuned to only the narrowest of bandwidths. While we can see and interact with gross objects, we perceive only a tiny spectrum of what is actually here. As a species, we've spent most our history blindly groping in the dark. I recently watched a TED talk by a cognitive scientist named Donald Hoffman. Hoffman explained that, evolutionarily, our senses are only tuned to focus on what immediately impacts our physical survival. In other words, we have evolved to see only a fraction of what's actually there. Only the greatest of mystics and seers, those rare souls who managed to take possession of their minds and turn their senses inward, have been able to glimpse the Infinite that has always and ever pervaded, enlivened and illuminated all beings.

If you were to ask me when I was growing up what I wanted to be and do in life, I'd have answered something respectable and at least halfway "cool", such as being a writer and artist. Which I, indeed, became. But there was something far greater that I craved and yearned for; and to which I was destined to commit my life.

In short, I wanted answers. I wanted to understand life and to know the truth about existence; about who we truly are and why we happen to be here. I didn't realise how deep I was going to run with this and how, as I made each step along this not-so-often travelled wilderness, the path would miraculously appear beneath my feet at precisely the right time. I never once fell, for I was held and guided every step of the way.

From the time I was just a child, I had the overwhelming conviction that there was more to reality than could be perceived by the senses alone; and so much more to each of us.

"Take up one idea. Make that one idea your life—think of it, dream of it, live on that idea. Let the brain, muscles, nerves, every part of your body be full of that idea and just leave every other idea alone. This is the way to success."

Swami Vivekananda

The Motivation Behind Spiritual Seeking

Most human beings don't have a whole lot of time for spiritual seeking, particularly in our age of rampant materialism and atheism. It can be hard to explain the spiritual impulse to anyone that doesn't share it. The staunch materialist is likely to see it as either a goofy personality quirk or a self-indulgent folly (which, for some people, it admittedly can be, as we'll see).

I suppose, like many things in life, if you don't have it, you can't really understand it. At its purest essence, it might be described as a fire within the heart, whether a tiny spark or a blazing inferno, and it cannot be ignored lest we lose something of our own heart and soul. Furthermore, it's not something that can be manufactured at will. It's either there or it isn't—and, in all cases, according to the Vedantic scriptures, this spiritual openness is a result of positive past actions or karma.

That said, the spiritual impulse can often lie dormant as we become immersed in the demands and strains of material living, particularly in the early part of our lives. I believe that sincere spiritual seekers are drawn to spiritual enquiry out of an inner necessity. Usually that involves some kind of suffering; a pain that, like the grit in the oyster, over time, creates a beautiful pearl. A true seeker will have learned, invariably the hard way, that lasting satisfaction and happiness simply cannot be found the world of finite forms and passing experience. Instead, what we seek is nothing less than than the Infinite.

It's vitally important, however, that we never abuse that spiritual impulse—for it can be abused.

Once the spark is there, I believe that two basic motivations can then drive our spiritual quest. The first, lower impulse, is a subtle and insidious desire to fix our problems by boosting and inflating our self-image and ego. In other words, we adopt "being spiritual" as a new ego identity; a way of setting ourselves apart from others and, if we're honest, of feeling superior and special.

The second, higher impulse, is to transcend the ego altogether and to find who and what we *truly* are when stripped of all false identification and ego-based needs and desires.

These two approaches are diametrically opposed. It can take a great deal of self-honesty to determine which of the two underlies our motivation. The first leads only to continued bondage and the second, ultimately, to liberation.

My first taste of alternative spirituality was provided by New Age type teachings. For the longest time, and before the internet had become the behemoth it is today, this seemed the only accessible alternative to conventional religion. We happened to live not far from an internationally known spiritual community, populated by all kinds of spiritual types living in cool little Hobbit-type houses. The place itself is beautiful; perched upon the edge of an estuary and surrounded by pine trees. I enjoyed visiting, although I sometimes caught a whiff of spiritual elitism among the community itself; an aura of subtle superiority in certain residents as they trotted about imperiously with their yoga mats in hand.

That, in itself, served as a lesson to me. The sad truth is that spirituality can go hand in hand with a certain narcissism. In the West, over the past four or five decades perhaps, spirituality has fused with personal development to such an extent it can often be hard to differentiate where one ends and the other begins.

It's a perilous combination. If, whether consciously or unconsciously, we find ourselves using spirituality as a means of boosting and enhancing our ego; of making ourselves into a "better person" and overcoming our sense of incompleteness by elevating our ego and self-concept then, I have to say, we may be abusing it. The idea of being a "spiritual person" is just another ego identity and, believe it or not, a "spiritual ego" can be just as noxious and self-defeating as a regular ego, if not more so.

Heck, I know of a phoney spiritual teacher whose life is a mess and who positions herself as some moral and spiritual authority because whatever she says "Spirit" speaks through her. She manipulated her poor partner by prefacing pretty much whatever she tells him with the words, "Spirit says...". He blindly accepted that, too, and more fool him. Such people are not uncommon in the spiritual scene and should, frankly, be avoided at all costs.

That may sound judgemental, but it's only meant as a cautionary note of discernment. You absolutely must keep your wits about you on the spiritual path. Ruthless and unflinching honestly must employed at all times, or else, rest assured, your ego—or somebody else's—will lead you on a merry little dance. It's a terrifying possibility, but, believe me, you *don't* want to spend decades thinking you're getting closer to enlightenment when all you're doing is fortifying an impenetrable wall of false conceptual identities and spiritual lies around your ego-self.

It's a pitfall we're all liable to succumb to at some point or another, particularly in the initial stages of our journey, and I was no exception. I had quite a damaged sense of self. I truly felt that I wasn't quite good enough as a person; that I wasn't a fit for this world and that, no matter how hard I tried, I could never make things work. Spirituality offered a new and much better identity.

Fortunately, somewhere along the line, by sheer grace, I was led from seductive yet dubious dualistic, ego-centred teachings to legitimate spiritual teachings. Accordingly, I began to shift from desiring a better, more enhanced ego to wanting to transcend ego altogether and know the *real* Self behind it. Instead of trying to use God to get what I (or, rather, my ego) wanted, I began to yield to that universal Intelligence and offer myself as an instrument for God to use. We're here to realise our divinity, our essential Oneness with our Source; not to attempt to use it as some kind of wish-fulfilling cow.

It takes a degree of spiritual maturity to get to that point. Fortunately, as the old adage holds, when the student is ready, the teacher appears. I confess it took a few years before I was ready and able to see through the spiritual materialism pervading the "Mind, Body, Spirit" bookshelves. It was only then that my true motive became clear. I simply, deeply wanted to understand the nature of Reality and my place in it.

Instead of trying to use God to get what I wanted, I began to yield to that universal Intelligence and offer myself as an instrument for God to use.

"If you correct your mind, the rest of your life falls into place."
Tao Te Ching

Truths and Half-Truths

The early days of my spiritual quest saw my focus was scattered far and wide. Although raised Christian by default, it didn't really speak to my soul. While I can now see their upsides in terms of devotion, I generally found the Abrahamic religions closed, narrow and out of step with the times; somewhat archaic relics of a bygone age.

As a teenager, New Age books provided an exciting alternative, offering glimpses of truth while feeling more positive and life affirming. Much of the New Age literature has its roots in Theosophy, as established in the late 19th century by the infamous Madame Blavatsky. Blavatsky, who some argue was a curious dichotomy of visionary and conwoman, drew liberally from ancient and purer sources, including Vedanta. That's why rivulets of truth ran through the New Thought and New Age movements, albeit contaminated by a lot of ignorance, misinterpretation and unfortunate cultural influence.

When the ancient teachings of Non-duality were mashed with the duality inherent in Yoga philosophy, we end up the pervasive notion that what we are is a "lower self" that must be merged with a "Higher Self" in order to be free. A half truth can be worse than a lie, particularly in spiritual matters, for the resultant confusion can potentially waylay seekers for a lifetime. Sometimes, however, a half truth is all that we have to go on, at least initially; and, fortunately, it's often enough to at least get us into the arena.

The idea of fixing up the ego self, of "perfecting" the person, is certainly a tantalising one (particularly for the ego itself). At one point, I pursued life coaching and even got a qualification to be coach others. I figured, hey, maybe this is how I can help others. It took only a couple of cases before I saw the inherent limitation in the approach. While getting what you want, or what you think you want, is hardly the worst thing in the world, such happiness tends to be short lived. The moment you fix up one part of your life, your career say, it's highly likely another part of your life, whether health or relationships, will take a tumble.

It's impossible to beat the system. Duality will always be duality and the attainment of perfection is ultimately impossible at this level. While we can, and should, strive to do what's right and to live well, to be successful and set and attain appropriate goals in line with our dharma and life path, the ultimate solution to our problems does not lie in simply rearranging the outer circumstances of our lives.

Our lack of happiness in ourselves is a spiritual malady, brought on by universal ignorance and, therefore, the solution is a spiritual one. I set aside the life coaching stuff almost the moment I started it. It was a nice idea, but it wasn't the path for me. I still hadn't got the spiritual side of things sussed. I needed to do that and, like a man obsessed, I simply would not relent until I had.

Our lack of happiness in ourselves is a spiritual malady, brought on by universal ignorance and, therefore, the solution is a spiritual one

"You show your worth by what you seek."
Rumi

A Spiritual Treasure Trail

It's probably no surprise that, over the years, I amassed a veritable library of spiritual books. I'm grateful to just about all of them, because each was probably just what I needed to read at the time. That said, there are precious few I'd wholeheartedly recommend now. The ones I would tend to be the ancient and timeless classics; works or revelations so divinely inspired that any attempts to better them in the intervening centuries has failed.

For a while, I explored Buddhism and felt a particular affinity with Tibetan Buddhism and elements of Zen. I particularly liked the work of Tarthang Tulku, from the Nyingma tradition and found his series on Tibetan meditation to be excellent. I also found value in the gentle, insightful writings of the late Vietnamese monk Thich That Hanh. I also once had the pleasure of seeing the Dalai Lama deliver a live talk and have always held him in the highest esteem as a true shining light in the world.

As it turned out, however, Buddhism wasn't enough for me. I have an enormous respect for it, particularly the Dzogchen and Mahamudra traditions, which appear to recognise our basic nature as Awareness. The basic problem, however, is that Buddhist teaching on the ultimate nature of reality can be contradictory depending on who you listen to and often lacks, in my view, coherent logic. With so focus on negating the emptiness of the phenomenal world, it fails to provide the necessary understanding of the underlying Reality out of which the forms and appearances arise. The recognition of the emptiness of name and form is an important aspect of Self-Knowledge. It is not, however, the ultimate Truth. For who or what is it that *knows* the emptiness?

From Buddhism, I gradually ambled closer to Vedanta, which

would be my ticket to freedom. I didn't take the direct route, however. Back then, if you'd asked me what Vedanta was I'd likely have shrugged my shoulders. In the West, it largely remains the greatest secret in the spiritual world; genuinely ancient yet hidden in plain sight and accessible only when the seeker is truly ready for it.

One of the stop-offs on my way to Vedanta happened to be Eckhart Tolle. Even some non-spiritual people may be familiar with his name, for he became something of an unassuming spiritual rockstar following the publication of his book "The Power of Now" in the late Nineties. I remember picking up a copy, reading a little, and then, for whatever reason, losing interest and setting it aside. While the structure is perhaps a little disjointed, it's a good book. It wasn't until a friend began raving about it several years later that I went back to it and gave it another shot. The second time round, it had much more impact. I guess, by that time, I was ready for it.

Eckhart is an interesting guy. He attained enlightenment while in the throes of a terrible depression and crippling existential despair. Subsequently, he's spent the rest of his life teaching and attempting to guide others to liberation as well. Ironically, the tools he teaches aren't the tools that led him to his own breakthrough, which was more or less a spontaneous and life-changing epiphany. There's a lot of merit to what Eckhart teaches, although I don't, personally speaking, know anyone who has attained actual liberation just by reading his words and attending his toe-curlingly expensive seminars. I'm not saying it's not possible, for he seems genuinely cognisant of who is he and there is much merit to his work, but it didn't happen for me.

As with so many of the teachings I was devouring, there was just enough to satisfy me for a little while, but, before long, I got hungry again. Something within compelled me to keep exploring and, by God's grace, the further I ventured with my spiritual explorations, the deeper I was led. From Eckhart, I discovered

Adyashanti, a former Zen monk who, like Tolle, teaches a kind of mashup of Vedanta and Buddhism, seasoned with a few other influences. Again, I found him to be a good teacher and his work was helpful at a certain point in my life, although it wasn't enough to ultimately seal the deal.

I kept on going. The more than I studied, learned and contemplated, the closer I felt I was getting to the ultimate Truth. After a few years of immersing myself in these teachings and what gets pejoratively termed "Neo Advaita" (a decontextualised repackaging of some of the core concepts of Advaita Vedanta), I was now convinced that I was not my body, mind or ego but the pure Awareness or Consciousness in which these components and the entire world was experienced. Bit by bit, this knowledge took root in my mind and heart and, the more it did, the more I knew that I was on the right track.

Something still wasn't clicking, however. The knowledge was there, certainly, but I didn't quite know what to "do" with it. As I continued this game of spiritual hide and seek, I knew I was getting warmer and that's why I kept persevering.

I would experience tremendous spiritual epiphanies from time to time, whether in meditation, in nature, or just walking down the street. Suddenly and rapturously, my ego identity and all sense of being a limited little person would vanish and be subsumed into a vast, panoramic sense of pure, all encompassing Awareness; a shining light without boundary and without beginning or end. The sense of limitlessness and bliss accompanying these shifts was off the charts. Nothing worldly, not the greatest of sense pleasures nor the grandest of ego indulgences, could compare to it in any way.

That's why I knew I must have been doing something right. The more doors I was opening, the more doors appeared, beckoning to be opened.

"Within the prison of your world appears a man who tells you that the world of painful contradictions, which you have created, is neither continuous nor permanent and is based on a misapprehension. He pleads with you to get out of it, by the same means by which you got into it. You got into it by forgetting who you are and you will get out of it by knowing yourself as you are."

Nisargadatta Maharaj

I Am That

By this time, Amazon was more than just a rainforest. The advent of online shopping made it far easier to acquire niche spiritual books and to browse the reviews for helpful suggestions. That was what led me, one day, to a striking black-and-yellow book titled "I Am That: Talks with Sri Nisargadatta Maharaj".

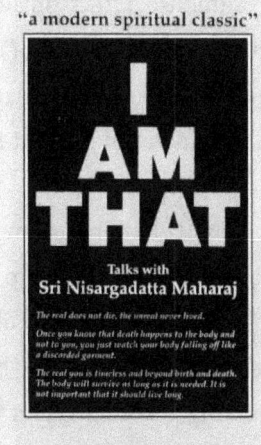

You'll find no shortage of seekers who consider this weighty paperback a watershed moment in their spiritual journey. While most start out reading books such as "The Power of Now", "I Am That" represents a move from primary to high school in terms of spiritual literature. It also served as my grand opening to Advaita Vedanta. While Nisargadatta wasn't a traditional Vedanta teacher, he was a liberated soul who used some of the language and concepts of Vedanta to share the most powerful and transformative of all knowledge: Self-Knowledge.

I immediately knew that I'd found the solution to my "problem of self". It confirmed the realisation that I didn't have a diminished self, after all. I had an imposter self; a case of mistaken identity.

I spent a whole year devouring this book. Highlighter pen in hand, I filled the pages with fluorescent ink as I came to any sentences that particularly jumped out at me, and there were no shortage of those. I found myself in awe, for it seemed to me the highest and purest distillation of spiritual knowledge that I'd ever come across. Just reading Nisargadatta's simple, powerful, direct words had an immense effect on me. They blasted my mind open to the increasing recognition of a deeper, transcendent, yet ever-present, immanent reality that was—Me; the *truth* of Me: simple, direct, pure Awareness; that fundamental ground of being in which all of reality appears.

I read a few other Nisargadatta books but none had quite the same impact on me, although they did help cement some of the key themes and provide a little extra sustenance.

From there, I discovered the deeply beloved Indian sage Ramana Maharshi, initially through David Godman's book "Be As You Are: The Teachings of Ramana Maharshi". Ramana's core message was the same: specifically, the key to liberation is coming to know the true I, the true Self, and to sever our deep rooted self-identification with the body, mind and ego. The latter is the source of all our suffering, as I was by now very much aware. The key to freedom is the shifting our sense of identification to a far vaster, greater and truer sense of Self.

In the words of Nisargadatta:

"The way to truth lies through the destruction of the false. To destroy the false, you must question your most inveterate beliefs. Of these, the idea that you are the body is the worst. Realise that what you are cannot be born nor die and, with the fear gone, all suffering dies."
Nisargadatta

"You do not need to leave your room...
Remain sitting at your table and listen.
Do not even listen; simply wait.
Do not even wait; be still and solitary.
The world will offer itself to you to be unmasked.
It has no choice.
It will roll in ecstasy at your feet."

Franz Kafka

Day of Bliss

Before we go any further, I'd like to tell you about the day, in my late twenties, when I thought I'd reached enlightenment.

I got up one sunny Spring morning, stepped outside and felt as though I'd been touched by the hand of God. Everything came into sharp focus and all I could see around me was beauty and wonder. Colours were suddenly pronounced and vivid; sounds sweet and melodic. The simplest of things—the turquoise sky, the way the trees, shrubs and flowers in the garden swayed in the gentlest of breezes, the feeling of warmth as the sun bathed my skin—all captivated me in a state of bliss.

Nothing had changed outwardly. It was just a day like any other. What I was seeing hadn't changed in any way, but the *way* I was seeing it had radically shifted. I felt like I was experiencing life for the very first time. Everything seemed indescribably beautiful; each sight a panorama of perfection, every motion a dance, and every sound a symphony of joy. The melodious sound of birdsong, the traffic passing down the road, the fragrance of the spring flowers and the simple miracle of my own body and its ability to breathe, and to see and smell, touch and taste, was an utter revelation to me!

It was all so perfect. Why hadn't I realised before how truly *wondrous* and *beautiful* life was?

Not that I was even thinking about it as such. Like a pristine forest lake, my mind remained still, translucent and reflective. There may have been stray thoughts passing here and there like fluffy clouds drifting across the sky, but thought itself seemed like an unnecessary indulgence. My mind had been stunned into a state of quietude, allowing the beauty and divinity of all things to reveal itself.

I realised that when the mind's stream of compulsive internal chatter ceases, all desires and fear, and all sense of lack, unease and insufficiency vanishes along with it. The concepts of past and future seemed like meaningless abstractions, and all my so perceived "problems" dispersed into irrelevance.

I sat drinking tea and looking up at the sky, my mind and senses absorbed by an ineffable bliss. Some mysterious doorway had somehow opened me to the immense beauty and divinity not only around me, but within. For amid this internal quietude, I felt my entire being flooded by a profound radiance, love and joy.

Feeling utterly whole and complete, I knew that nothing was lacking and nothing could ever possibly be lacking.

This sense of wholeness and deep-rooted satisfaction enveloped me with a rising wave of gratitude and love; love for all the beautiful sights and sounds around me, love for the body and mind registering them, and above all, love for the light and bliss that seemed to shine at the very core of my being, radiating out in all directions, encompassing all that I could perceive and more.

I instinctively knew that this, whatever it was, wasn't something that had been *added* to me in some way. This light and bliss had always been within me; ever present and ever shining like the sun, even if hidden by layers of cloud.

What a revelation that was! I didn't need to *do* anything in order to manufacture, manipulate or orchestrate this bliss. I didn't need to seek it or run after it like a child chasing a butterfly with a net. It was already there as the very core of my being; as the essence who and what I am—and it was divine; it was God, and it wasn't separate from me in any way.

I could sense this divinity not only within myself, but all around me in all things; in the taste of the tea, the rustling of the leaves, the sun sparkling upon concrete and the swish of my dogs' tails as they came up to me looking for attention; the light in their eyes no different to the light I experienced within myself.

As I noted in my journal later that day, "Everything was sublime. Everything made my heart dance. I felt at one with everything and filled to overflowing with a deep, deep sense of peace, joy and *aliveness*."

I lost all interest in doing anything that day. I just wanted to *be,* and to enjoy this current of bliss pervading my mind, heart and senses. Although I was a regular meditator and chanted mantras every morning, I was certain that what I felt wasn't the result of any *doing*. It wasn't something that had been added to me by some practice, effort or mental orchestration. Rather, I experienced it a sense of pure, naked *being*...which I later learned the ancient Vedic scriptures refer to as *Sat-chit-ananda*; existence, consciousness and bliss; which happens to be the very nature of the Self.

This epiphany lasted most of the day, even as I went about my daily activities. At one point, I wondered if anyone would notice anything different about me, because I literally felt the light shining from the pores of my skin and merging into the ocean of light I sensed all around me. I felt connected to everyone and everything in a way that went far beyond a mere intellectual understanding of Non-duality. I experienced a blissful sense of unity and love for all things; a love as indiscriminate as that of the sun shining upon the earth.

Funnily enough, nobody noticed anything different about

me. Not that I wanted or needed any such acknowledgement. But I did wish I could somehow transmit what I was feeling to everyone. Heck, if everyone knew just how beautiful this world was, and how blissful the light of our own being happened to be, there never again be a harsh word spoken or the slightest trace of conflict, anger or resentment.

I'd never felt as wonderful my entire life; which made it all the more painful when this remarkable state of consciousness began to contract and fade. If I recall, one of the triggers was talking to my partner at the time, who was in a particularly grumpy and argumentative mood. Like a bubble bursting, the bliss began to fade as the mind kicked back into gear, again drudging up its old habitual defence mechanisms and patterns of reactivity. As the mind began churning out a stream of internal monologue once again, the ego reasserted itself and the bliss dried up.

The moment I felt it starting to fade, I began trying to grab hold of it, to manipulate and take possession of it. The sublime sense of effortlessness and non-doership that precipitated the epiphany was replaced by a crude straining and striving.

Over the next few days, I was able to tap into that bliss for a few moments here and there, but the overwhelming reorientation of reality was gone. I was back to being Rory, the person; back to seeking, striving and trying to make life work for me. I'd gotten my "enlightenment" only to lose it again.

It wouldn't be for another few years that I'd realise what I'd experienced wasn't enlightenment. Enlightenment isn't an experience, as such. Enlightenment is the realisation that we are *That which experiences*; and that regardless of the experience we're having, be it good or bad, we are always and ever whole, complete and free.

What I'd experienced was a spiritual epiphany; an elevated state of consciousness in which, like a polished mirror, my mind became clear, pure and reflective, allowing me to taste Reality as it actually is. This altered perception of Reality was totally contrary to how we ordinarily experience the world through our habitual mind-based prisons of separation, lack and doership.

The reason I wanted to share this is to highlight that true joy, freedom and bliss is to be found *within* us. It's the essence of what we are.

I'd experienced many wonderful things in the world of form and objects, including moments of great happiness, pleasure and triumph. But nothing I'd ever experienced as a result of worldly gain or sensory experience ever came *close* to the bliss I experienced just sitting in my garden, doing nothing but enjoying the light, radiance and wonder of my own existence. This didn't come from outside of me. It came from within me. It *was* me.

That day made me realise that I was on the right track. I had committed myself to Self-Realisation; to enlightenment, as ostentatious as that sounded even to myself. I was meditating and practising self-enquiry daily, savouring the wisdom of Nisargadatta and Ramana Maharshi and trying to let it soak into the deepest recesses of my mind. It now seemed to be working!

Freedom, I realised, wasn't something to be acquired and attained "out there" in the world of objects, forms and experiences. As the Bible states, "the Kingdom of Heaven is within." That day seemed to be a confirmation. The solution wasn't out there in the world, and it never was. The solution was within.

Part 3

VEDANTA - MAP TO FREEDOM

"The destruction of delusion does not require any weapon. All that is involved is the lighting of a lamp."

Swami Dayananda Saraswati

How to Attain Enlightenment

2011 was the year I discovered Vedanta. In retrospect, I'd been drifting in the spiritual wilderness somewhat, intent on my destination, but unsure how to ultimately get there. Now, by divine grace, I was about to be given as clear and concise a map as I could ever dream of.

It had been a rough year for me health-wise, so when friend invited me away for a week's holiday in the sun, I jumped at the chance. After all, living in Scotland, the sun was something I never saw quite enough of. I first had to renew my passport as I hadn't been abroad in several years. As I was getting all of that arranged, I hopped onto Amazon to see if there were any good books I could take along as a holiday read.

Still deeply enamoured with "I Am That", I was keen to find another Nisargadatta book, even though the others I'd read hadn't quite hit the spot.

At this point, I'd had some exposure to Neo Advaita. Neo Advaita teachers generally cherry pick the key concepts of Advaita Vedanta and wax lyrical using all kinds of inspiring "pointers". The core message is always there; the fact that what we truly are is pure Awareness. Unfortunately, because they only know select elements of Vedanta, they lack a complete teaching. So, while Neo Advaitins have the first and last steps of the ladder (acknowledgement of the individual and the Self; Awareness), the middle rungs are completely missing. A ladder with missing rungs in the middle is unfit for purpose and somewhat dangerous to boot.

The material of Eckhart, Adyashanti and others had definitely helped me to a certain point. I'm grateful for having come across their work and believe it does have value. I'd gotten to the point where I intellectually understood that my true Self was Awareness and not the body, mind or ego. The problem was, however, the knowledge was not sticking. I still found myself experiencing that all too familiar sense of lack and limitation associated with being a person in samsara.

Such frustration will be familiar to many seekers: "I know that I'm the Self, pure Awareness, but somehow I'm still reacting and feeling like the same old person I've always been." That's a sign you really need a teacher to help get you unstuck and, quite possibly, a better teaching. That was precisely what was about to happen for me.

There I was, clicking through Amazon's "You Might Like" algorithm, when one particular book jumped out at me, no doubt in large part due to its bold and uncompromising title:

"HOW TO ATTAIN ENLIGHTENMENT".

Wow, I thought, that's not certainly beating around the bush.

I clicked on the book, which was written by an American teacher named James Swartz, and had a scroll through the contents section. I was immediately impressed by the sheer breadth and scope of the topics covered. Clearly this wasn't just another Neo Advaita book of well-intentioned yet frustratingly vague waffle. It seemed substantial, complete and, skimming the first few pages, I immediately connected with the direct way it was written. There were a handful of reviews by that point; all unanimously positive. I didn't need to think twice. I was sold—and so was the book! I clicked a button and, a few short days later, the book arrived. I packed it alongside my shorts, sandals and sun lotion.

Before I knew it, I was lying on a sun lounger by the pool, baking in the Spanish sun and immersing myself in what I quickly realised was the most impactful and life-changing book I had ever read. Yes, "I Am That" had stopped me in my tracks and had an enormous impact on me. "How to Attain Enlightenment", however, filled in all the missing blanks, many of which I hadn't even knew were there. This was Vedanta in its purest form, as taught by a teaching lineage stretching all the way back to the visionary sage Adi Shankara in the 8th Century.

As I would soon learn, Vedanta offers a map of Reality itself. It leads us from the gross to the subtle; from the world of the visible to the all-pervading Formlessness that the Sages have, for millennia, sworn to be our true essence and nature; both the source and substance of all that is.

This book had its work cut out living up to its extraordinary title. Fortunately, it did not disappoint. I felt like I'd come home; and that someone had finally managed to connect all the dots for me. It was exhilarating: enlightenment while getting a suntan! Surely it didn't get much better than that?

"In the whole world there is no study so beneficial and so elevating as that of the Vedanta. It has been the solace of my life—and it will be the solace of my death."

Arthur Schopenhauer

Vedanta

I can't express the relief I felt upon realising that all the pieces had already been tied together—not by some hotshot new author looking to sell overpriced seminars, but by an ancient system of knowledge thousands of years old. For, as the book's author, James Swartz, unequivocally declared, this wasn't "his" teaching. Rather, it was the pure distillation of a system that has been liberating minds for millennia.

The mystery of reality and the end to human suffering had already been sussed *thousands of years ago!*

That was a real newsflash moment for me. It's only comparatively recently, say in the past century, that Vedanta has been available publicly and in English; and even then it remains the spiritual world's best kept secret. Despite the efforts of luminaries such as Swami Vivekananda at the turn of the twentieth century, Vedanta didn't export nearly as well to the West as, say, Buddhism.

Remarkably, I'd been around the spiritual block for a number of years and knew people who had been seekers for decades on end yet who didn't know a thing about traditional Vedanta. Nevertheless, its core message inextricably pervades numerous other systems, trickling down to inspire and shape countless teachings over the centuries, including religions such as Buddhism itself, which borrows many of its core concepts from the Vedas in which Vedanta has its source.

Whereas Buddhism lent itself to both export and a degree of secularisation, I suppose it's possible that Vedanta, as the core philosophy at the heart of Hinduism, seemed too enmeshed in Indian culture and theology to appeal to the uninitiated Western seeker. Such a person may take one glance at the various deities of Hinduism and dismiss it as a curiosity specific to India and not at all relevant to a modern day Westerner. That's a sad misconception if ever there was. What they don't realise is that the actual subject matter of Vedanta is timeless and universal: namely, the inner divinity of all humankind, all beings and all life.

Perhaps due to its relative obscurity outside of India, Vedanta has tended to be a last resort teaching for many. When aspirants eventually concede that Buddhism, Taoism, Neo Advaita or whatever other paths they've been diligently following haven't yielded the results they hoped for, they may eventually, hopefully, find their way to Vedanta. If they're then able to set aside existing preconceptions and approach the teaching and the teacher with the right attitude and with a suitably receptive mind, that's when the true magic happens.

This doesn't mean, however, that our previous spiritual education was any more in waste than the years of our primary or elementary schooling. I'd venture that Vedanta is university level spiritual education, and most people probably wouldn't be ready to jump straight into it without a little background experience.

The purpose of this book isn't to detail the ins and outs of Vedanta. My next book, "Enlightenment Made Simple" is intended as an accessible primer for beginner students. In the meantime, I suggest the book "Vedanta: The Big Picture", which I edited from talks by the great teacher Swami Paramarthanada of Chennai. My book "Bhagavad Gita: The Divine Song" provides a more comprehensive unfoldment of the teaching. I also, of course, highly recommend the aforementioned "How to Attain Enlightenment" by James Swartz and his subsequent overview titled "Essence of Enlightenment"; James also has a number of other superb titles. The remainder of this chapter provides a quick and simple overview. You may or may not be interested, although, if you've managed to get this far into the book, I imagine you'll be at least curious.

So, simply, what is Vedanta?

Vedanta is a means of knowledge intended to liberate the mind and remove existential suffering. Literally meaning "the end of Knowledge" (or the knowledge that ends the need for any further knowledge), Vedanta is the distilled knowledge of the Upanishads; end portions of the ancient Vedas, the world's oldest extant spiritual texts.

The Upanishads, the oldest of which were composed thousands of years ago in ancient India, are said to be revelations intuited by the sages of old. Seeking to understand the mysteries of existence, these mystic seers devoted their lives to deep meditation and contemplation. Their findings were then recorded in incorruptible Sanskrit mantras and passed down unchanged through the millennia.

These revelations of truth are threaded by an overarching theme: the inherent oneness and divinity of all life.

According to the Upanishads, the entire universe is but the product of a singular, eternal Non-dual Reality. Referred to as Brahman, or the Self, its essence is Existence itself and its nature pure Consciousness or Awareness. Underlying and pervading the entire creation, this Self is the sentience lending life and consciousness to all the seemingly separate beings, much as the sun lends the moon its reflected light while itself remaining changeless.

According to Vedanta, life's highest goal—and the key to liberation—is to realise our essential oneness with this universal and all-pervading Consciousness/Awareness.

Existential suffering is born of misidentification alone; of falsely superimposing our sense of self, of "I am-ness", onto the adjuncts of the body, mind and ego. By mistakenly assuming ourselves to be nothing but a finite body/mind/ego entity, we adopt the limitations and the sorrows of these vehicles, which are, sadly, infinite in number.

The end of suffering, which is called *moksha*, liberation, or enlightenment, comes through Self-Knowledge alone. This Self-Knowledge allows us to see past the ignorance that has kept us bound to matter and to reclaim the truth of our being as the infinite, limitless Consciousness that is the root and essence of Existence itself.

This is, of course, the same essential truth espoused by the world's great wisdom traditions all across the ages. Vedanta offers one of the clearest and most comprehensive maps to realising and actualising this knowledge. It begins by outlining the mental qualifications necessary prior to beginning our journey to Self-Realisation. It then outlines the three main stages of the teaching methodology.

The first stage is simply listening to the teaching. The second stage involves reasoning and resolving any doubts and confusion that might arise along the course of our study. The third and final stage requires steady, sustained contemplation of the knowledge until it unravels the any lingering knots of ignorance in the mind.

The end result? Freedom from the suffering caused by false identification with the aggregates of matter! We relinquish our identification as a limited little person subject to the ravages of time—which happens to be a strictly conceptual pseudo-identity, for where does the "person" you think you are exist other than as a thought in your mind?

Only by doing that can we reclaim our birthright as the limitless and eternal Self; the ever present and changeless light of Awareness in which all objects of experience arise and subside like waves upon the ocean of eternity. You might think of it as akin to the wave suddenly realising that it is, in fact, non-separate from the vast ocean.

I already knew the basic truth of my nature as Awareness before discovering Vedanta, but I'd never heard it elucidated so beautifully, so completely, clearly and fully. Reading James's book, I realised that Vedanta was nothing less than a science—a science of consciousness and a roadmap to that seemingly most elusive of things: enlightenment.

What a blessing that I had now been gifted with this knowledge. Whether I realised it or not at the time, Vedanta had changed my life forevermore.

"When the student is ready, the teacher appears."

Aphorism

I Meet My Guru

Over the course of the next year, I read and reread "How to Attain Enlightenment" several times until virtually every page was covered in highlighter pen and notes. I lapped it up with a mind ravenous for something substantial.

James, whose spiritual name is Ram or Ramji, had not only written a fantastic book, but created a jewel of a website called Shiningworld; a veritable treasure trove of spiritual knowledge. Along with questions and answers via years worth of correspondences with students, the site offered a significant amount of audio and video taken from James's seminars, much of which was free to download.

As I listened every single night, I quickly fell in love with James's pointed, down to earth and no-nonsense teaching style. Aside from the incredible breadth and depth of his knowledge, I found his "realness" and total lack of pretension deeply refreshing. He came across as a regular guy with no airs or graces, and no attempt to portray himself as some kind of exalted holy man who expected his followers to bow down and worship the ground he walked. Wholly unafraid of being provocative, James never hesitated to call a spade a spade, was unashamedly un-PC and also outspoken with regard to some of the more controversial teachers out there—earning him not only detractors but some outright enemies.

Personally, I found it impossible not to love him, for he was uproariously funny and filled with sparkling energy, vigour and joy. Most importantly, whereas most of the modern teachers I'd encountered tend to sit and waffle for hours, delivering meandering talks that might be inspiring but also lacking in substance and cohesion, James spoke and wrote with exceptional clarity and power. Here was a man who not only had the virtue of a real and cohesive teaching—but damn, he was brilliant at teaching it.

James happened to be the disciple of a famous and revered teacher named Swami Chinmayananda; a true force of nature and a trailblazer who revitalised interest in Vedanta during his illustrious lifetime. His other main teaching influence was another of Chinmayanana's students, Swami Dayananda Saraswati.

Having attained liberation in his thirties, James had spent the intervening years honing his teaching skills and, around the time his book was published, his fame and reputation in the field of Vedanta were growing significantly.

It was a year after discovering his book that I first emailed James and began occasional correspondence, and a year after that before I met him in person. The moment I did, at a yoga centre in the Andalusian mountains of Spain, I was awestruck by the way the light shone from his eyes as he looked at me. I think that was the moment when I realised that he was my guru and I his disciple.

Until this point, I don't think I'd ever met a liberated soul. Yet, I could readily see that, even as Consciousness filtered through the lens of a personality (in James's case the self-confessed "redneck guru from Montana"), James's identity rested in the Self and was unbound by the adjuncts of body, mind and ego. Devoid of pretension in a way some found disarming, James was definitely the teacher that I had been waiting for.

Fifteen-odd years of being a spiritual seeker had brought me some illumination but also a whole lot of ignorance and misconception too. I find the modern spiritual scene an unfortunate mishmash of profound truth and blatant untruth. Indeed, the two can be so inextricably woven that all that's left is an avalanche of erroneous notions—notions that not only fail to lead to enlightenment, but which may actively push it away.

Sometimes, a gentle tap on the shoulder is not enough. Sometimes you need a teacher with an edge; somebody who doesn't take any shit and is willing to sandblast you free of all the ignorant notions accrued over many years of haphazard, misbegotten seeking (in the nicest, kindest possible way, of course).

Unfortunately, many spiritual teachers are either knowingly or unknowingly compromised by the income they hope to derive from their endeavours. After all, they have their market to consider. Rather than sharing hard truths and being willing to tell people what they may not want to hear (which is often precisely what we need to hear), they sugarcoat things and oversell the promised, yet by no means guaranteed, benefits.

Not so long ago, I saw Eckhart Tolle advertising a course on manifesting your desires. Despite the overt commercialisation of his output, I like Eckhart and always assumed he knew what he was talking about. The fact is, however—and this is a hard sell to the Western consumer-mined seeker—enlightenment has *nothing* to do with manifesting what you want. How could it? Liberation means freedom from slavery to desire. That comes from the realisation that what we truly are is already free of all want and lack. A true teacher's job is not to pander to the student's avaricious ego. Their duty is to reveal to the student the part of them that does *not* want; the inner core of Being that's ever desireless, whole and free regardless of what's happening at an external level.

There's only one desire encouraged by the Vedantic scriptures and that is the desire to be free. A burning desire for enlightenment is an essential prerequisite. Without it, we're unlikely to devote the necessary time and energy to its pursuit. That's where most people stumble on the spiritual path. If we don't value freedom above all else, if it's but one desire sandwiched between a dozen other worldly desires, we're never going to get far spiritually speaking.

If you detect a note of frustration there, it's because I'd struggled through the spiritual wilderness for over ten years by this point. All the while, I'd gotten just enough to sustain me; enough morsels of Truth to keep me going and looking for more. But I was tired of the half-truths and the mixed messages. I didn't want someone telling me what I wanted to hear simply because they were manoeuvring toward the up-sell. In spite of all my reading, reflecting and meditating, and in spite of my occasional spiritual epiphanies, I was still stuck identifying as a person; this well-meaning, earnest guy named Rory who had tried so hard to make his life work but who kept on hitting roadblocks.

Break out the violins if you like, but prior to journeying to Spain to meet James, I'd had a rough time of it. I'd just escaped, or perhaps been jettisoned from, an ill advised and rather toxic relationship (of course, I didn't realise it was toxic until the eventual postmortem). My health remained a challenge and, after years of fruitless work, my first novel, "Eladria", was picked up and released by a publisher—only to drop off the cliff in terms of sales. Somewhat embarrassed, and also irked by the publisher's lack of effort in promotion, I never contacted them again and...well, they never contacted me.

All in all, events had served as a bitter reminder that even achieving the things you most dream of in life—love! Success! Recognition!—are no guarantee of happiness in any lasting measure.

There's no solution to the game within the game itself. Our real problem is not life, but ignorance; in the form of our false notions about who and what we are. We've become locked into identification with a false pseudo-self; a wanting, needing, grasping self that, driven by a basic sense of lack, is forever seeking love and happiness outside of itself.

The only solution is for us to know, with the entirety of our being, what we *actually* are. Then we can't help but love ourselves because we find that we, ourselves, are the very source of all love, of joy and of bliss. Sounds so easy, I know, but it takes a heck of a lot of energy, effort and dedication to take that knowledge and use it to break loose the shackles of both heart and mind.

By now, I was certain that the only hope for true and lasting happiness was enlightenment. James seemed a living testament to that. I'd never met anyone quite so free and at ease in himself. Even though he happened to be suffering significant heart issues when I first met him, the light simply shone from him and he never let pain or discomfort diminish that light in any way. I was also blessed to meet and get to know James's wife, Sundari, an excellent teacher herself, who had also liberated herself by the light of Self-Knowledge and who shone with a remarkable radiance, warmth and strength. I was getting to see firsthand what it was like to live with a mind established in the Self and the impact you could then have upon the world and other people. Nothing can inspire and motivate quite so much as being in the sphere of what Vedanta calls a *jnani*, or knower of the Self.

The challenges I'd experienced in the preceding months and my determination to exit samsara had led me to a time of sublime blessing. Convinced that freedom was there for the taking, I was no longer hankering for success *in* the world as much as freedom *from* the world. I was committed to the path. The only question was, as I wrote in my journal one night: "Do I have what it takes?"

With James in Malaga, 2019.

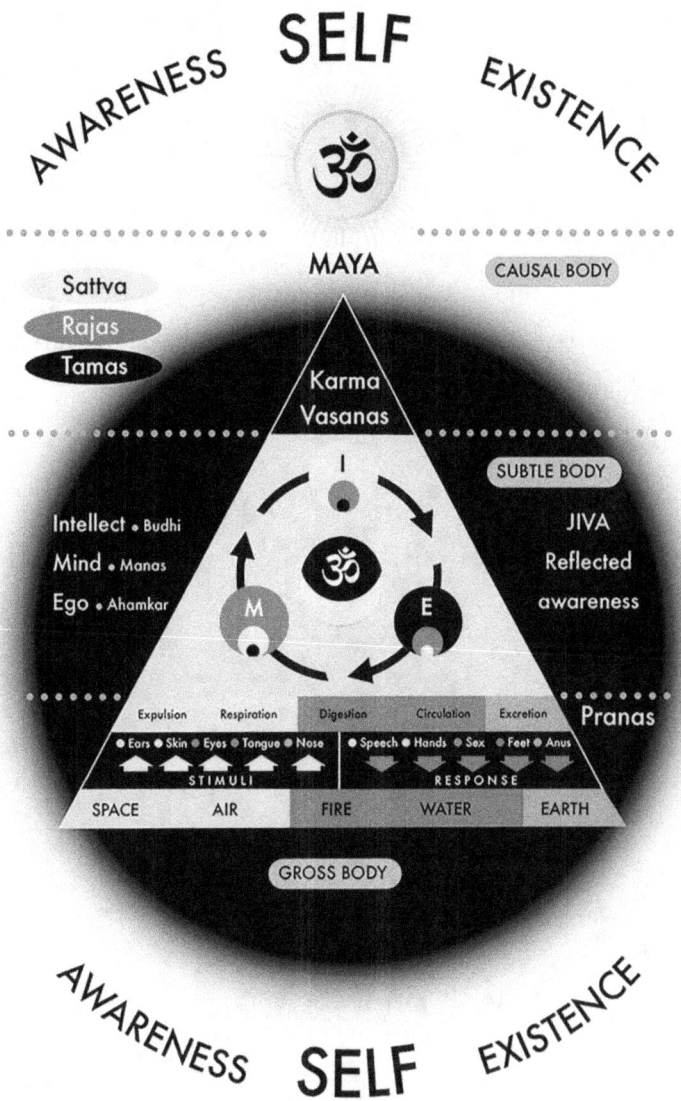

The Vedantic map of Reality. Chart designed by James Swartz.

"There is someone who looks after us from beyond the curtain.
In truth, we are not here. This is our dream."

Rumi

The Highest Blessing

Although it may not always seem like it, particularly if you happen to read the daily headlines, the Vedantic scriptures are resolutely clear on this point: we are lucky to be born human!

Although, like animals, we are conditioned with instincts, impulses, desires and fears, human beings are also gifted with the faculty of intellect and discrimination. We have the unique ability to reason and contextualise our experience; to think, reflect and to choose our own path. This has its downside, of course. Humans tend to suffer far more than other creatures because of our ability to think, imagine and judge. As Seneca put it, "We suffer more in imagination than in reality."

Fortunately for us, the very same mind capable of causing such unnecessary sorrow is also the gateway to what Vedanta declares to be life's highest goal: enlightenment, liberation or freedom from the wheel of perpetual birth.

Although, for many people, the mind is little more than a sorrow generating mechanism, if used properly, it can be our portal to freedom and an end to suffering. If that's our goal, however, we need to be clear that it's not going to "just happen". We need to work hard to *make* it happen. We do that by ensuring that our mind is an appropriately fertile field for the seeds of Self-Knowledge to take root and grow. The condition of our mind is ultimately what determines success or failure; whether we get liberated or remain stuck in the perpetual suffering of samsara.

Over the years, I'd met people who'd been at the spiritual game for not just years, but decades. Some had been at their spiritual practises, whether spiritualism, Buddhist chanting, TM, or whatever else, for forty-odd years, diligently in search of

Nirvana or enlightenment—and still not an inch closer to their goal even after all those years.

To me, such a predicament seemed horrifying. The thought of fruitlessly seeking enlightenment for decades and being no closer to finding it struck a cold fear into my heart. Given the elusiveness of this particular goal, perhaps I'd have been better quitting while I was ahead and conceding to a life of blind hedonism?

But nope, I knew I wasn't a quitter.

I vowed to do whatever it took to get to the end of this whole spiritual quest. I wasn't looking to gain anything from enlightenment. I'd already shed the erroneous belief that enlightenment conferred some kind of Midas touch; that everything I touched would automatically turn to gold. It would be nice if it worked like that, but I'd already relinquished such magical thinking. Quite the opposite, enlightenment is less a case of addition and more a process of subtraction. Specifically, we lose the sense of being a separate being beset by all kinds of personal problems and sorrows.

I was willing to go all out and do whatever I could to make this teaching work for me. While desire is ordinarily frowned upon by most spiritual paths, it so happens that Vedanta encourages the desire for freedom as a necessary prerequisite, and it was one I had in abundance.

The text we studied at my first Vedanta seminar in Spain was Vivekachudamani by Adi Shankara (roughly translated as "The Crown Jewel of Knowledge"). In one of the opening verses, Shankara highlights the aforementioned value and blessing of a human birth. An even greater blessing, he goes on to say, is a human birth plus the burning desire for freedom. That's something that's quite rare even among spiritual people. Of all the spiritual people you know, how many are actually, genuinely and bona fide *committed* to attaining enlightenment? The ultimate blessing is, according to Shankara, not only the gift of a human birth and the desire to attain liberation, but access to both the teaching of Vedanta and a qualified teacher.

Once those are in place, by the grace of God and the merit of past karma, we have both the opportunity and the means to fulfil life's highest purpose.

I may not always have felt that life was going my way, but I now realised that, from the spiritual vantage point, I was profoundly blessed—and if you happen to be reading these words, I have a suspicion that you are, too.

Above: Casa Mayor, beautiful venue for my first Vedanta seminar. Left: James getting teach to teach, 2013. Below: James and Sundari shining bright.

Humans tend to suffer far more than other creatures because of our ability to think, imagine and judge. As Seneca put it, "We suffer more in imagination than in reality." Fortunately for us, the very same mind capable of causing such unnecessary sorrow is also the gateway to what Vedanta declares to be life's highest goal: liberation or freedom from the wheel of perpetual birth.

"He who has a why to live for can bear almost any how."
Friedrich Nietzsche

I Found My Purpose

My week in Spain at James' seminar was a watershed moment in my spiritual journey. The decision to take the plunge and attend a seminar in person after having spent a year immersing myself in Vedanta through books and audio recordings was precipitated by heartache and a deep disillusionment with life and love. It was a blessing to not only be in the presence of more than one jnani but to meet a great many other seekers, all truly lovely people and some of whom I'm still good friends with. The venue was also incredibly beautiful; a small yoga centre perched on the mountains of Andalusia with a breathtaking view of the valley beneath.

As we got cracking with the teaching, what I realised, above all, was that this was my dharma, my true purpose in life: not trying to be successful in worldly terms or trying to get others to love and validate me—but pursuing moksha; the only true and lasting freedom from suffering and lack.

While the pursuit of moksha was traditionally viewed as a legitimate life path in India, let's just say that a modern Western viewpoint would deem the pursuit of enlightenment as wacky at best. That's much to our detriment, of course. I realised that while I might be committed to life's highest and noblest purpose, it wouldn't be looked upon with any legitimacy by the majority of people, entirely wrapped up in worldly concerns as they are. I'm fortunate that my family not only understood (I think) but also supported me and, in my mother's case, even shared that goal. While I certainly had a few spiritual friends, most of the friends my age were uninterested in spiritual matters and saw my "hippie" tendencies as eccentric and possibly charming depending on how charitable they were feeling.

Alas, I'd spent too many years concerned about what others thought of me. Indeed, Rumi once noted:

> "Half of life is lost in charming others. The other half is lost in going through anxieties caused by others. Leave this play. You have suffered enough."

I now had to be true to myself and to do what I knew mattered most, regardless of what others thought. I'd suffered enough. I wanted an end to it and that's precisely what Vedanta offered. I had faith in the teaching and, by divine grace, I'd found someone who could teach it with skill and precision; and, crucially, without diluting or distorting this age old means of knowledge.

As I mentioned before, Vedanta works in three stages. The first is called *shravana*, a Sanskrit word which means "listening". You simply sit yourself down and listen as the teacher starts at the beginning and works their way through the various teaching texts.

It's important to listen with what the Zen practitioners call a beginner's mind. After all, it's impossible to fill a bucket with fresh water without first emptying the bucket. One of the problems with spending years or decades hopping from teaching to teaching is that we can develop a certain arrogance. We think we know more than we do when, in fact, we're still blighted by ignorance. After all, if that weren't the case, if ignorance had been eradicated, we'd no longer be seeking and would be completely content and satisfied with life and ourselves exactly as we are.

I knew that wasn't the case for me. I was still tremendously dissatisfied! Fortunately, I had the humility to set aside everything I thought I knew; and I simply sat and absorbed what was being taught. It all made such perfect sense, too. This was a teaching that covered all the bases. It wasn't simply vague, flowery talk about our nature as Awareness. It filled in all the missing blanks and examined the nature of not only Consciousness, but the appearance of the world and all the forms therein. This was a teaching that unfolded the big picture and I really needed that in order to contextualise everything.

The second stage of Vedanta is called *manana*, which comes from the Sanskrit word *manas*, referring to the mind. This stage involves careful reflection upon what is being taught and then systematically resolving all questions and doubts. One of the great things about Vedanta, and the reason it actually works, is that it isn't based upon blind faith in doctrine. While we do require a certain degree of faith in order to take the plunge and invest the necessary time in getting to grips with the teaching, it's not necessary or advisable to simply take the teacher's word for it.

Rather, we have to reason through every part of the teaching. If we stumble upon any part we don't understand or can't process, it's essential to work through that with the help of the teacher. Doubts are a silent killer and will sabotage the efficacy of the teaching like nothing else. I seemed to have a solid grasp of what was being taught and didn't have any real doubts, although there were certain aspects of the teaching that wouldn't be entirely clear to me for some time.

Some people found it more of a struggle and I could sense they were having difficulty processing even the basics of the teaching. I found that I was often able to help them. This, in turn, helped me to deepen and refine my own understanding. It also let me see that I had a knack for sharing knowledge in a simple and accessible way, perhaps aided by my education in Social Science and having developed the skill of gathering, evaluating and presenting information.

The final stage of Vedanta, *nididhyasana*, is all about digesting that knowledge. This stage follows logically from the first two; first we acquire the knowledge, then we resolve any doubts or misunderstanding we have about it. The final step is to fully internalise and actualise it. It's not enough simply possessing an intellectual understanding of spiritual truth; this knowledge must be turned to firm *conviction;* until we feel and know the truth of it with the entirety of our being. It's only then that Self-Knowledge—specifically the knowledge that we are not a limited body/mind/ego but the boundless Awareness in which they appear—can transform suffering into liberation.

This crucial final step is all about application. We gradually assimilate the knowledge gained from the teaching through steady and systematic contemplation and reflection. It may take considerable time and effort. Ignorance comes hardwired into the very framework of the psyche. Furthermore, our senses are directed outward and, so, most people are so consumed by worldly objects—not to mention the inner phantasmagoric creations of the mind and ego—that they have no real way of knowing who and what they truly are.

While the first two stages necessitate the careful guidance of a teacher, the last stage is a solitary one. We've been given the knowledge and have, hopefully, fully understood and grasped its importance. Now we have to apply it to the mind over and over again until, finally, it neutralises the mind's ingrained layers of ignorance and conditioning. This is obviously not a one-time task. In fact, it's a war that must be continually waged for as long as it takes. Then, by God's grace, the glorious day will dawn when we realise that the struggle is finally over; the inner conflict is resolved, and there is nothing more to do.

I now had to be true to myself and to do what I knew mattered most, regardless of what others thought. I'd suffered enough. I wanted an end to it and that's precisely what Vedanta offered.

"Paradise is where I am."

Voltaire

Airport Epiphany

My last day in Spain was one I will never forget. I shared a taxi ride from the yoga venue to the airport in Malaga with two of my fellow seminar attendees. Both had early flights whereas my flight wasn't until much later in the day. I'd knew I'd have to wait around the airport for the best part of the day, but it was still the best option as sharing the taxi cut the cost of travel by a third. It wasn't long before I said goodbye to my new friends and tried to figure out a way to pass the next several hours.

After a while, I got tired of sitting around the airport and decided to take a train ride to the beach. Alas, I couldn't find a place to leave my suitcase and it was too early to check in, so I ended up dragging it along everywhere with me. It was pretty cumbersome, too, because I'd brought along a sleeping bag and pillow as I'd been sleeping on the floor of the yoga studio. Hauling my case along behind me like some kind of tourist snail, I stopped at a cafe for lunch, wandered around for bit, and then headed back to the airport.

At that point, with several hours still to go before my flight, I decided I might as well use the time wisely. One of the things you'll maybe notice about seminars or workshops is that, while people pay rapt attention while the teacher is speaking, the moment there's a coffee break or things end for the day, the silence is shattered by a cacophony of noise and chatter. I didn't especially enjoy the sudden eruption of noise because I was invariably spellbound by the teaching and wanted to hold onto it and bask in its glow rather than have it to disperse into mundane chitchat. That's actually one of the best things that anyone can do. It's not enough simply to listen. The magic happens when we spend significant time contemplating the teaching, allowing the mind to absorb it like a sponge soaking up water. That, in fact, is the essence of the third stage of Vedantic practice: steady and sustained meditation upon the knowledge. Without this crucial final stage, the knowledge will never penetrate deep enough to neutralise the manifold layers of ignorance pervading the psyche.

One of the topics Ramji had explored in his unfoldment of Shankara's Vivekachudamani was called *samadhana*, which means the single-pointed concentration of the mind; in this case, upon contemplation of our nature as Awareness. This ought to be a sustained, laser-like focus capable of mercilessly tuning out all preoccupations and distractions. As I sat on a bench outside the airport rereading some of my notes, I suddenly became obsessed with the idea of samadhana. I had plenty of time to spare, so I just continuously kept my mind focused upon the knowledge, "I am Awareness".

Now, it's extremely difficult fixing the mind upon Awareness because Awareness is subtler than the mind. There are certain tricks, however, such as shifting our focus from awareness *of* objects (whether the gross objects of the senses or the subtle objects of the mind) to *that* which is aware of them.

So, as I gazed around at the buildings, the vehicles, the people passing by or up at the cloudless sky, I kept asking myself, "How do I know this? How do I perceive this? What is perceiving?"

The only appropriate answer was, simply: Awareness. Awareness. Awareness.

The more I kept my mind rooted in awareness of my own Awareness, the more it became absorbed, until, suddenly, something seemed to shift.

I recall looking up and seeing aeroplanes moving across the turquoise sky; diffuse contrails in their wake like spiders' webs woven across the heavens. The sudden realisation dawned upon me that *my Awareness was just like the sky*; vast, all encompassing and, of itself, formless. All the objects I was perceiving—whether the outer, physical forms relayed by the senses or the subtle forms of any thoughts drifting across my mind—were all just like these little planes moving across the endless and impassive expanse of sky.

I reached into my case, grabbed my notepad and pen and began scribbling furiously as I sought to process this realisation. I still have those very notes and what follows is a condensed version of what I wrote as inspiration flooded my being; the essence of what I'd learned from a week of intensive Vedanta retreat.

I'm still not entirely sure whether it's wise to be sharing it here. It's a free-flowing, disorganised sprawl of flashing ideas and revelations, mixed with self-directed advice. It might make sense to you, or it might not. I felt compelled to share it, nonetheless, because it represented an important turning point in my spiritual journey.

This was the moment that I suddenly, truly, realised that:

I am the Awareness—the baseline Awareness—in which this all, ALL, arises.

All the forms of the world, the people, places, objects and sensory experience, are just temporary phenomena arising and subsiding in Awareness. None of it affects Awareness. It's all the same. Jivas [individual beings] come and go like clouds in the sky, programmed by their gunas [constituent natures] and vasanas [conditioning]. So many different phenomena passing across the sky. None of it is in any way personal, because there is no person.

Everything is experienced as objects arising upon the screen of Awareness. They depend upon Awareness. Awareness doesn't depend upon them.

I finally get it. I'm so grateful, so blessed to have had this teaching, this opportunity. So amazing!

James told me to "take it easy". Consistently apply the Knowledge. Cease this false identification with the body, and with self-image and ego.

Constantly bring it back to Knowledge of Awareness and objects arising; the two categories of existence—Reality and appearance; Formlessness and form.

The objects are in Me, I am not in them, nor bound by them in any way.

I AM AWARENESS.

Awareness is everything—the only Reality. All else is just appearance in Awareness. Awareness gives life and sentience to the subtle and gross bodies. Awareness grants sentience just as electricity blesses a lightbulb with light. The lightbulb itself is inert, and so too are the body and mind without the presence of Awareness.

The crux of liberation is differentiating Awareness from that which appears in it.

I am Awareness and not the jiva; not the thoughts, the feelings, circumstances or experiences—all of which are objects arising and subsiding.

"Person" is just a concept. Like all things, the personhood is just an appearance in Awareness and all this is being taken care of by Ishvara [the God principle].

What need be done? Except to rest and abide in Awareness, as my very nature.

Allow all the prarabdha [karma] to come; the thoughts, the feelings, the judgements, the fears and wants and hurts. Allow the mental formations to arise and subside. Pay them no heed. Allow it to exhaust. Dismiss the vasanas by knowing I am Awareness. See them as objects arising, and I am that in which they arise.

Let Ishvara do its job. Leave it all to God. I'm not doing anything anyway. Let God control everything and relax.

I AM AWARENESS.

I lack nothing. As Awareness, nothing can be added to me and nothing can be taken away from me. I have no need now to chase after objects—people, situations, relationships, love, success, validation or approval—because none are lasting. What can be gained can be taken away and if I am attached to and dependent upon them, I will suffer.

I chased—I obtained, temporarily—I lost—I suffered.

I suffered through misplaced identification. Oh, how I suffered! Only, I never suffered; not the Real I; the bird on the branch impassively observing the other bird as it pecks away at the fruits of life [a metaphor from the Mundaka Upanishad]. It was never going to end well for the ravenous bird as it manically pecked away at life. Kentucky Fried Chicken. Man, how awful. My seeking in the world did nothing but fry me; it added nothing but pain.

The ego is driven by a feeling of incompleteness. This incompleteness is due to ignorance of the nature of Awareness. This ignorance is channeled into chasing objects. Samsara city. I got sucked into this samsara, again and again and again.

How does knowing I am Awareness change things?

Nothing is lacking.

I cannot be any more, or less, than I am now.

It really doesn't matter what other people think or what they say or do or don't do. Because they are no more real than the little ego "me"; they're just driven and controlled by their karma. How can I get upset, angry or take anything personally? When there isn't even a person, for me or for them.

This world is a puppet show! Controlled by Ishvara and illumined by Awareness. How much free will do these jivas really have? How much free will did my jiva have? How can I take the show seriously? How could it ever have been remotely serious?

It's time to stop comparing my jiva to other jivas in the show. Let him be translucent. Be a ghost in this world and simply let Awareness shine. I know what I am.

This moment as seen from the perspective of Awareness: A light allowing images to spill onto and fill this screen of Awareness. Objects arise and subside; all kinds of sensory experience both gross and subtle; always temporary and fleeting in nature, but the light revealing them is eternal.

Freedom is separating limitless Awareness from the objects appearing in it and resolving all the objects into Awareness with the Knowledge:

I AM AWARENESS!

I ended this stream of consciousness contemplation with a quote from Vivekachudamani which seemed to sum the entire truth in just a few words:

"I am whole and complete bliss, free from lack and always present. I am everything that is."

Later that day, I added the following:

*"The Awareness contains all.
It's so simple, isn't it?*

*Stick to this Awareness through Samadhana—
Keep the mind fixed on Awareness as much as possible."*

That's precisely what I did, and I was filled with the most incredible bliss and joy; and the sense of being utterly immutable and indestructible.

Somehow the ego, the sense of being a separate little person, shifted to the periphery of my consciousness and the Awareness, which had habitually been ignored and unacknowledged, shifted to the foreground.

With a still and luminous mind, I simply watched with wondrous joy all the comings and goings at the airport, including my own body as it moved about, waited around, drank coffee, got onto a plane and was transported back home. Free, fresh and alive, I felt as vast as the sky; and all the objects I happened to witness were just like the clouds beneath. Everything just moved through me in a divinely perfect flow of experience. I, as Awareness, remained the unchanging constant while all the forms around me changed and shifted in kaleidoscopic beauty. None of it affected me in any way; that much was clear to me. What a blessed relief; nothing in this world could change me, could hurt me, could touch me, the *real Me*, in any way.

That night, as it was a late flight, I stayed at a guesthouse in Edinburgh. Unusually for me, I hadn't checked the customer rating before I booked and it was only later that I saw the unremitting cascade of one star reviews. Even for cheap accommodation, it was something of a shithole; something you wouldn't really expect these days in the heart of the city. There were no staff on site and it took me an age and several phone calls to figure how to get in and access my key. My room was dirty and dilapidated with peeling wallpaper, no curtains and damaged blinds which did little to keep out the glare of the streetlights. There was a tap that didn't work, a broken bed and piles of dust, dirt and debris around the headboard. I don't think I'd ever seen such an unloved and unclean hotel room.

I'm fastidiously clean by nature and like orderly environments. This time, however, I didn't care one little bit. It did nothing to impact the joy and bliss I was experiencing as my mind remained merged in luminous Awareness. Everything around me was somehow a source of delight, even my grubby room.

If anything, the imperfections struck me as humorous; a reminder that nothing in this world of form is perfect, while the Awareness revealing it is, in essence, forever pristine pure. Everything seemed so unutterably beautiful to me. Every single form and object filled me with wonder because it all seemed such a miracle; this incredible world of forms appearing in the unending formlessness that was Me; that was my true nature (and the true nature of all beings).

Interestingly, although thoughts would still roll across my mind like waves in the ocean, albeit lesser in number and with far less opacity than I was accustomed, I didn't seek to understand or label this epiphany. Something fundamental had shifted, yet I didn't think "Wow, maybe I'm finally enlightened". That may have been because there didn't feel like an "I" there to *be* enlightened; not in the sense people usually think of "I". There was just light; just an expanse of all pervading, ever shining Awareness—no person, no individual to "be" enlightened. Knowledge alone had shifted things; the knowledge that I was

Awareness and not the instruments of body, mind and ego appearing in Awareness.

The "person", I realised, happened to be a convenient fiction cooked up by the mind to enable us to interface with our environment. Life is a "let's pretend" of the highest order, although virtually every human being is so immersed in the game that they completely forget it's just role play. It would be quite funny if it weren't so tragic, because all human suffering is rooted in this delusion; in the mistaken assumption that we're all limited little entities bound by time, physicality and mortality.

Yet, from the perspective of the Self, even that is fine, because nothing in the phenomenal dream can affect it, can affect Reality, in any way whatsoever. That's why freedom is already attained and doesn't need to be sought or strived for. All that's necessary is the knowledge that we are not who we take ourselves to be.

Vedanta had finally revealed that truth to me. My heart sang with joy and swelled with an endless ocean of gratitude. Everything I'd ever experienced in life, all the good things and the bad, all the pains and heartaches, had led me to the realisation that it was *all absolutely fine as it was*. God was everything, everywhere, and I was non-separate from this Infinite Light.

"The greater danger is not that we set our aim too high and we miss it, but that we set it too low and we reach it."

Michelangelo

I Got It, I Lost It…

For the next several days, this knowingness that I was simply pure, shining Awareness stuck with me. I felt like I was effortlessly floating along on a filament of light, sustained by pure grace and watching in wonder as life spontaneously, delightfully unfolded around me, completely under the control of God, and my body and mind along with it. I don't think I told anyone about this radical shift, although one or two people noted that I was "glowing", and strangers would look at me in the street and sustain eye contact for notably longer than is normal. In truth, it felt as though *everything* was glowing, for the entirety of existence seemed to shimmer with light.

And then, much to my dismay, the glow began to fade.

It didn't happen all at once. Rather, it was over the course of a few days. That wondrous bliss? It began drying up as my mind, like a computer rebooting, began defaulting to its old patterning. I could sense the focal point of my identity pivoting from Awareness back toward the ego, which hopped back from the background and resumed its place front and centre. I didn't want to admit what was happening, even to myself. I'd felt like I'd been admitted to Paradise only to be kicked out when my ticket expired.

I was pulled back into ego-identification mode largely by the unprocessed pain and heartache following my breakup weeks before I headed for Spain. I hadn't thought about it much while I'd been away, but gradually those thoughts began intruding upon my serenity, and I found myself involuntarily dragged back into compulsive rumination.

Oh, I'd had breakups before and they're never fun, but this one had been more like an evisceration. In my defence, you do experience significant cognitive dissonance when somebody shifts from "love bombing" to treating you like you're absolutely nothing to them in the space of just a few weeks or months. My mind was trying to understand and to make sense of something which just didn't make sense. Rather than seeing objectively, however, I was left questioning my worth as a person. That, of course, was so totally, *ridiculously*, at odds with the knowing that I was the Self; I was non-separate from God—and therefore, like all beings, innately of unquestionable and inalienable worth.

Over the days that followed, the sense of wholeness and freedom I'd experienced following my seminar steadily slipped away. In its place, the sense of being a person returned; a person who'd opened his heart, which took a fair measure of courage and trust in itself, only to have stomped on. That and the dispiriting non-event that was the release of my first novel a few weeks earlier conspired to create a sense of failure. What's more, I'd somehow internalised the poisonous notion that failure is personal; that if something doesn't work out it's not even so much a case of experiencing a failure as *being* a failure. What a terrible, self-defeating belief to harbour; what a source of sorrow and grief—and not at all true, either.

It's sobering reading my journals from the time, which veer from God intoxication and bursting with inspiration and joy to the eventual realisation that, as I wrote at the time: "I feel like I've lost it." At the same time, I knew how ridiculous that was. "WHO feels like they've lost WHAT?" I wrote in the next sentence, continuing: "Awareness is still here. It can't go anywhere! It's free. I am Awareness, therefore I am free. These thoughts have nothing to do with who I am."

I tried valiantly to reason my way out of it, but there was no quick fix to healing this particular grief. There had been no closure. The relationship had been coldly and clinically terminated when I dared to challenge the way I was being treated. All communicated was immediately severed. I was told, "I don't untie knots. I cut them off." That wasn't the way I operated; it wasn't the way I conducted relationships. I sought harmony, and if not harmony then understanding; and if not that, then at the very least the ability to part on anything approximating good terms.

The shift I experienced by immersing my mind in the knowledge that I was Awareness was genuine and life-changing. It wasn't, however, something that could or should be used to sidestep the unresolved feelings in my heart. Tempting as it is, spiritual bypassing is never a viable solution. Unless you deal with and resolve what's eating you up inside, it's a safe bet that it'll eventually end up devouring you from the inside out.

It's not necessary or even possible to perfect the mind. Yet, if we ever hope to attain liberation, it is vital that we cultivate a sufficient mastery of our own mind; or, like a carriage without a driver, we'll find ourselves dragged uncontrollably off course and subject to all kinds of calamity.

Vedanta highlights the need for both control of the senses and the cultivation of steady, mature and dispassionate mind; a mind that isn't too disturbed by unprocessed emotions, attachments and unresolved karma. Without that, try though we might, Self-Knowledge simply won't, and can't, stick. We may have an intellectual understanding that our true nature is Awareness, but that won't translate to liberation.

In short, if we don't sort out "our stuff" prior to enlightenment, we'll have to do it afterward, or else we'll be catapulted back to square one.

It was a tough lesson. The most important ones often are.

"Do not weep; do not wax indignant. Understand."
Baruch Spinoza

The Spiritual Achilles Heel

Each of us has a spiritual Achilles heel. It's vital that we are aware of it—or else it'll sabotage our efforts toward enlightenment without fail.

We all have a weak spot; an area of ignorance, attachment or addiction which, like an elastic band, binds us and, whenever tugged, forcefully snaps us back into samsara. It's not until we have a sufficient degree of self-awareness that we can begin to manage it and, a large measure of time, effort and vigilance, eventually move beyond it.

Most of our sticky issues fall into one of two categories: success and love. Success encompasses all kinds of worldly desires and ambitions; ranging from basic security and the pursuit of wealth, to career, status, reputation and power. This becomes the entire focus of many people's existence. Alas, "success" is a constantly shifting benchmark and money and status are absolutely no guarantee of satisfaction and happiness, as the rich and famous often lament (usually to not much sympathy from the rest of us!). Wealth and success are a legitimate pursuit for most; indeed, the initial stages of life require wealth and security. Like a narcotic drug, however, they provide hits of pleasure but in the long run come with the potential for addiction and all kinds of mental and emotional agitation.

Most spiritual seekers tend to understand the inherent limitations of materialism. It's rare, although not impossible, to find a seeker of enlightenment still hung up on money, wealth and power (although this can, sadly, be the downfall of some gurus once they get a taste of power). We spiritual types are more likely to have issues with love. We may feel we lack love, we aren't loved enough, or we have issues with the need for approval, validation and acceptance. This is an extremely common problem.

I was fortunate to be blessed with a loving family, although from a young age I was acutely aware of not fitting in with others and feeling different, disconnected and somewhat alienated. In order to feel some sense of belonging, I learned to compromise who I was in order to play a part and pretend to be like others. As a particularly sensitive child, I then grew up with self-esteem issues and, like many people, came to believe that my worth and value were determined by what others thought of me.

That's nothing but a recipe for disaster when it comes to relationships—and was, indeed, my own particular spiritual Achilles heel. When we don't feel whole and complete in ourselves—which is, as it happens, the basic problem of samsara—we feel compelled to seek that from others. What a precarious endeavour it is to seek happiness outside of ourselves; and one that invariably leads to disappointment and disillusionment. After all, anything that can be gained can be lost again.

As long as we remain hung up on security and love issues, our values will naturally be split—and a split value can be fatal when it comes to liberation. While on the one hand, we may value and be committed to enlightenment, we also still have a value for worldly attainment; whether that might relate to success, money, career or relationships and so on. We basically want to have our cake and eat it. We want enlightenment but we also want to keep chasing certain things in samsara on the side. This clash between the desire for liberation and the compulsion to keep pursuing our worldly addictions and compulsions is often enough to scupper our hopes for freedom.

Nobody really wants to hear that unfortunate truth, and most mainstream spiritual teachers will never admit to it; because, frankly, it's unlikely to sell books and seminars. The market savvy spiritual teacher knows what sells—and that tends to be the promise that people can get everything they want and *more!*

When it comes to enlightenment, however, our value for that must be *so* strong that it supersedes all other values. Split values ("I want this...but I also want that!") divide the mind, dampen our motivation and muddy our priorities. I think that's why it took so long before my long spiritual journey actually yielded fruit. I wanted liberation, yes, but I also felt I needed a relationship; I unconsciously felt as though I was only of worth and value if I had someone to reflect that back to me. I was also still trying to make a career for myself, if only to justify my existence to the wider world—something we all, consciously or not, feel compelled to do in this day and age. Both of these attempts met with a whole lot of frustration and disillusionment, but it was the love issue that caused the most pain.

It's not an easy one, to be sure. The desire for love and connection is hardwired into us. Furthermore, our senses are externalised and automatically hooked onto the world of objects. So, it's only natural that we tend to seek the love we need from outside of us. Even when, say, a spiritual teacher tells us that joy only comes from within and that there's an inexhaustible supply of love right inside of us, it can still be hard recognising that and tapping into that inner supply.

It may take considerable work to go against the grain and shift our focus from without to *within*. Yet that's precisely what we must do if we ever want to experience genuinely lasting happiness and unconditional love. Object-based love certainly brings its fleeting joys and pleasure. However, relying upon a finite, ever-changing world of duality for lasting satisfaction only ever guarantees perpetual disappointment and sorrow.

The world ain't designed for that! It's designed to wake us up!

"Why struggle to open a door between us when the whole wall is an illusion?"

Rumi

Relationships and the Love Issue

I've always been an avid people watcher. Not in a creepy way, thank you very much, but more of a romantic "artist sitting outside a Parisian cafe watching the world go by and looking for inspiration" kind of way. Indeed, you can learn so much about life simply by observing people.

I was sitting in a restaurant one evening, a number of years ago. I happened to catch sight of a youngish couple nearby, and it was then that I realised one of the most important things you ever need to know about romantic relationships.

Without doubt, this particular couple were near the beginning of their romance because they seemed loved up to a factor of a hundred and ten. Each was gazing lovingly into the other's eyes, their full attention focused in laser beam precision, listening with rapt attention to every single word, eyes twinkling as they beamed and laughed at each little joke or witty remark.

It was a far cry from an older couple sitting just a few tables down. This pair, perhaps in their late sixties, sat in what seemed to be abject misery, barely so much as acknowledging the other's existence. A protracted silence lingered as they laboriously ate their meal, seemingly having run out of conversation decades previously.

This truly is a world of duality, I mused.

Going back to the young couple, one thing struck me in particular. Each was experiencing the joy of their own love reflected back at them. It was as though, in the mirror of their beloved's eyes, they could see the light of their own being. It was present in their partner's smile, in their laughter and the uninterrupted attention and presence they were receiving. Heck, the building could have been burning to the ground around them and I'm not sure either one of them would have noticed.

That's when I realised one of the primary reasons we seek love and engage in romantic relationships. We want the other person to mirror our own beauty and light back to us; to reveal to us what we perhaps can't see in ourselves—that higher, deeper aspect of our nature which is just pure love.

Most people, hostage to ignorance, are incapable of seeing those things in themselves. It's a sad fact that many have a dysfunctional, even abusive relationship with themselves (and by "themselves" I mean the ego's appraisal of itself; for most people don't have a clue who they really are and that, of course, is the core problem). I certainly did for a number of years.

When you can't find the love in yourself because toxic conditioning has distorted your self-image and ignorance prevents you from realising the magnificence of what you truly are, of course you'll seek it by proxy. You'll be on the lookout for anyone or anything that promises to give you even the most fleeting taste of what you lack—and, often, you'll be willing to pay a hefty price for it (for there's always some kind of price).

We all naturally want to love and be loved. That's because, whether we know it or not, love is our nature. If, however, we can't see and appreciate our own inner light, we'll happily rely upon somebody else to reflect it back to us. Just like the young couple in the restaurant, they might do this in a thousand different ways; from the way they look at us, the attention they pay us, to the compliments, the promises, the sweet gestures and even just the time they're willing to spend with us. It's no wonder the initial stages of a relationship are so delightful. When we "fall in love", our brains release a cocktail of hormones and chemicals, leaving us aglow with a narcotic euphoria. Some people call this "new relationship energy." It's nice—nice, that is, while it lasts.

Of course, like anything in duality, there's no up without down, no hot without cold and no day without night. New relationships progress into established relationships; if, of course, they make it beyond the honeymoon phase. Flash forward forty years and that loved up young couple could well find themselves like the bored and apathetic older couple eating their meal in stony, disinterested silence.

It took me a number of years to get wise to the game. It was only then I realised that, while it has its upsides, the seesaw of romantic love wasn't altogether as wonderful as the love songs promise—and is, alas, no solution to the basic problem of inner lack. It took a fair bit of bruising before I got to that point.

For me, the imprint of my adolescence, a lingering self-esteem issue and longing for a sense of belonging and connection fuelled most of my romantic relationships. I learned to project confidence, and some considered me good-looking, so I never really had to be the one to put myself out there, initiate things and thus risk rejection. I just waited for people to come to me, and they invariably did. Accordingly, I fell into a number of relationships where I perhaps should have exercised better discernment.

The immediate upside was knowing that somebody liked me and wanted me; and this assurance was an instant salve for a shaky self-esteem. What I was often doing, however, was trading who I really was in order to become an idealised image of what somebody else wanted me to be. That isn't healthy. In fact, it's probably the definition of codependency. Back then, however, I was driven by forces that I didn't understand or even recognise.

At least part of the issue came down to values. When you don't share the same values as the majority of people; if you happen to see the world, life and love in a different way to most, it can be hard to find anyone you truly connect with and you may feel a little vulnerable sharing who you really are. Relationships, however, must be based upon shared values, or there won't be enough glue to hold things together once the novelty wears off.

Something of a shapeshifter by nature, I tended to adapt to who I was around; to be who the other person wanted me to be. I didn't consciously know that I was doing it. It just became a mode of being. Looking back, I wasted so much time in the earlier part of my life trying to project a facade of normality in a misplaced bid to prove that I was loveable. I'd somehow internalised the belief that *different* equals *bad* or *inferior*. In fact, I should have celebrated that difference, because that's the way that I, as a person, was made; the way I was meant to be.

Accordingly, I found myself in a number of relationships that weren't particularly conducive to who I was or to my path in life. It's perhaps little wonder they invariably ended before long. Each time that happened, it felt like a blow; when, in retrospect, I can see it as a blessing, for it was God rerouting me from situations that weren't right for me. It didn't help that I was probably looking for something that a relationship wasn't capable of giving me: the assurance that I, as a person, was basically all right and that I was worth loving.

That's not something we should be looking from another person. Our sense of self-worth and inherent wellbeing must always be self-bestowed. To place it in the hands of another invites tremendous insecurity. Maybe that's why I was always waiting for the wind to shift; for the other person to decide that perhaps I wasn't "all that" after all.

Fortunately, in time, I came to realise that romantic relationships are no solution to the problem of self lack. Far from solving all our problems, they actually come with their own set of problems. I'd always leapt into things with the expectation of finding unconditional love. That isn't something I think I ever experienced in romantic relationships; at least not in any lasting capacity. I came to realise that, for most human beings, relationships are transactional in nature. I'd had partners tell me "I'll love you forever" and "I'll always be there for you." At the time I believed them, because if someone tells you something like that you want to believe them.

The thing is, however, people will only love you as long as it suits them to love you; as long as there's a clear advantage to loving you. If circumstances change, or the relationship hits a rocky patch and begins causing more stress than satisfaction, it won't be long before the love dries up. When the scales tip and the relationship ends up being more of a hindrance than a joy, or somebody new and better comes along, you'll find the love has evaporated, and, along with it, all the promises of undying devotion, leaving you wondering if it was ever truly real in the first place.

The last relationship I was in brought me to an incredible realisation. It was disillusioning in the best sense of the word, for it finally blasted away all the illusions I had about the nature of what I thought of as "love". For once, I'd found someone that I actually had a lot in common with, only to realise that he was emotionally unavailable. He basically admitted that he didn't have feelings for me and was afraid he never would. I think most people probably harbour some deep, unconscious fear that they might be, at their core, somehow unlovable. To have it confirmed in actual words ought to be devastating, but I found it—liberating.

A bubble burst. I realised, once and for all, with absolute and irrevocable certainty, what the spiritual teachers of all ages had been saying throughout the ages:

Seek not outside yourself.

I'd been looking for love and validation from others even though, intellectually, I knew that I was the Self and, therefore, the source of all love. Until I had properly assimilated and integrated that knowledge, there was an incongruity between what I knew and the way I was acting; the latter driven, as it was, by unresolved karma and unhealed wounds—forces that were, for the most part, out of my control. Through ignorance, I was seeking love outside of myself—only to experience how finite and fickle such love can be—until finally, *finally,* that particular compulsion just died.

I didn't even have to do anything myself; it just popped like a bubble and was gone.

I no longer needed to seek love. It was already there; always. I could see so clearly that love was eternal. It was within me all the time, or it was nowhere.

I'm not sure if this realisation was perhaps quite as immediate as I'm making it sound. It may have happened more gradually over the months, but it nevertheless happened.

It was, I believe, the last vestige of my seeking anything outside of myself. Life is an inside job. All the love, the happiness and satisfaction are already within, if hidden by ignorance. Yes, it can be reflected by others and by conducive situations and experiences, but it always comes from nowhere other than our own Self.

I've always found the words of Sufi poet Rumi of great inspiration and insight, and I finally came to realise the truth of the following words:

"Your task is not to seek for love, but merely to seek and find all the barriers within yourself that you have built against it."

When the barriers began to fall, I saw how crazy I'd been chasing love in the wrong places when it was already all around me, all the time. I was never lacking in love. I was already adored by my family, my beloved dog, my friends, and so many souls I have connected with, however briefly, along life's path.

Love. It was all *love*.

I realised, above all, that love was my nature—and everybody's nature. Some people are capable of mirroring that love back to us, but many aren't. Indeed, there are a whole lot of cracked or dirt-covered mirrors going about the world. But even if someone cannot reflect love back to us, it doesn't mean that it isn't there. If you could just wipe the mind of all ignorance-induced thoughts, you'd be able to turn inward and see, perceive and feel it all around and within you, as the very essence of what we are as Consciousness.

When you understand the greater Reality, love is no longer a thing you seek to attain, but rather an immensity you perceive in and around you, everywhere, at all times. There's nothing to get from anybody else. All that you have is the desire to *give* love, because you *are* love. When you can see beyond the divisive barriers of the human mind, every single interaction is simply love receiving love. Even the people who hate you don't actually hate you; they hate a false idea they have about you in their mind. In actuality, everybody loves you because everybody ultimately loves themselves—and, since there's only one Non-dual Self, you are that Self!

Interestingly, I lost all desire to pursue romantic relationships. Relationships hinge upon our ability to match up our likes and dislikes with another person's likes and dislikes. That's what ultimately determines compatibility. It calls for varying degrees of compromise and, while compromise is a healthy thing to a certain degree, in the past I was willing to compromise far too much. I'm not saying that I would never have a relationship again, but the desire for it, and desire in general, in fact, is just not there anymore.

I'm now just myself without compromise. I finally found the ability to feel completely whole in myself and that truly is the sweetest thing. All of my seeking, and of all my gains and losses, joys and sorrows, ultimately lead me back to my Self and the realisation that *nothing was ever lacking.*

Incidentally, as a caveat, it's never entirely possible to know when *samsakaras*, or conglomerations of conditioning and psychological patterns, have really been eradicated for good. It's always possible for old patterns and pockets of ignorance to lure us back into samsara, often without us even noticing it. I experienced that a couple of times—thinking that I was free and didn't "need" a relationship, only to end up in one and find it triggered a lot of the old conditioning and patterns. As my guru's guru, the great Swami Chinmayananda said, "Eternal vigilance is the price of freedom."

You do, however, get a sense of when an old and constrictive karmic pattern has been released. Mercifully, it frees up a huge amount of psychic energy and life force which can then be directed elsewhere. As it happens, I knew precisely where to direct it.

When you understand the greater Reality, love is no longer a thing you seek to attain, but rather an immensity you perceive in and around you, everywhere, at all times. There's nothing to get from anybody else. All that you have is the desire to give love, because you are love.

"Life and death are of supreme importance. Time swiftly passes by and opportunity is lost. Each of us should strive to awaken! Take heed, and do not squander your life."

Dogen

A Matter of Commitment

Many years ago, I heard the following words spoken by Pema Chödrön, and they stayed with me ever since:

"Since death is certain, and the time of death is uncertain, what is the most important thing?"

This question is one we should each ask ourselves each and every day. It has a way of focusing the mind and cutting through the crap like nothing else.

Our time upon this earth is fleeting. We only have a finite amount of time to accomplish our goals. The question is, are we pursuing what is really and *truly* important to us? Or are we being swept along by the roll of past momentum, unconsciously living out of habitual reaction and focusing on things that don't ultimately matter?

So, what is the most important thing to you?

Why do you think you're here?

How can you make this lifetime truly matter?

The issue of values is a pivotal one, particularly for the spiritual seeker, who must navigate the world and deal with all kinds of mundane, worldly matters, while remembering that, ultimately, the most important of all goals is the pursuit of liberation.

At least it should be. For the sincere seeker, to prize anything less is to sell ourselves short and rob ourselves of our birthright. Please, never make the mistake that countless others do and waste your precious lifetime worrying about trivia when you can set your heart and mind on the highest of all attainments: freedom from samsara.

As Ramana Maharshi said:

> "Your own Self-Realisation is the greatest service you can render the world."

If you lack clarity with regard to your values, your motivation will be muddied and your actions muddled. All three are irrevocably linked. It's not until you're absolutely clear that liberation is your highest and most important goal, that you'll actually make that a priority—and it must *be* a priority. It's a gamble to leave it until later in life. After all, the future is guaranteed to no one. This moment, right here, is all we ever actually have. As the Zen saying goes: "If not now, when?"

I can't remember the exact point when everything came into sharp focus for me and I realised that I either had to go all IN with the enlightenment thing or else set it aside, forget about it and try to make the best of life.

I suspect a gradual series of events highlighted to me the fact that object-based happiness is the most precarious type of happiness. Continually chasing wealth, fame, love and various other attainments and trying to steer our outer circumstances into alignment with our likes and dislikes is a recipe for continual frustration. Whatever moments of happiness we do derive from such endeavours tend to be so fleeting they hardly qualify as happiness at all.

For instance, all my attempts to be a successful author, fix up my health and to find security, love and happiness in the world seemed only to lead to frustration and disappointment. Was I simply a failure at life? Or was I failing because I knew I wasn't taking the right tack? I knew, in my heart of hearts, that I wasn't here to attain worldly success. I never expected that I'd have anything in the way of money, fame and fortune and I was okay with that. I just wanted to be free, and I'd already been given the ticket to freedom. The question was, would I take advantage of that great blessing, or would I continue floundering around in samsara for a few more years trying as hard as I could to "amount to something"?

I knew that object-based happiness wasn't the solution to life's existential suffering. I also knew that—no matter what successes we attain in life, and in spite of moments of happiness and accomplishment—until we get to the fundamental problem, the dissatisfaction and emptiness remain. I'd long suspected that my path through life was not an "ordinary" one. One of the themes of my life had been having the courage and conviction to be true to myself and to walk my own path, regardless of what others thought.

I'd been shown the way out of this whole existential pickle. By the grace of God, Vedanta came into my life at just the right time and I actually already had the knowledge in my head. I knew the ultimate Truth. What I needed to do was get my mind under control and hold fast to that Truth; to contemplate it with relentless resolve until this knowledge converted to ironclad conviction.

That may, in fact, be the most important part of the entire spiritual path: taking Self-Knowledge and allowing it to saturate the mind and heart like a sponge soaking up water. It's only then it can dissolve away the seemingly endless layers of ignorance that have conditioned our thoughts, behaviours and responses for untold lifetimes.

This ignorance does not die willingly. It takes significant time, effort, commitment and perseverance to slay the dragon of ego identification. A lot of the Neo Advaita teachers state there is nothing to "do" because we are "already free". That's true at the Absolute level of Reality, but it's probably not true at the relative level. Superimposing the Absolute upon the relative does not automatically solve the problem. The mind is configured a certain way. It takes time to reorient it to this new operating system; one rooted in the simple yet radical knowledge that what we are is not the body/mind/ego apparatus, but the formless Awareness/Consciousness pervading and enlivening it.

Rarely does this sink in overnight. It may be adopted as an intellectual belief, but until that belief is converted to a fully integrated conviction, it won't translate to liberation.

Nope, there's no getting around the fact we need to get down and dirty in the trenches, because the mind will not acquiesce easily. It'll keep churning out the same old patterns of ignorance until we face it down and rigorously apply the knowledge "I am Awareness" and not the objects of Awareness. We have to do this over and over again.

This fundamental reorientation will likely require us to simplify our lives, follow the path that is correct for who we are, perform each action as an offering to the divine and accept the circumstances and happenings of our lives as they arise (while being willing to change them if appropriate).

Ultimately, everything in this virtual reality creation is conspiring to wake us up from the dream of ignorance and point us to the ultimate Truth that everything is God and we are non-separate from God.

A life of service, devotion and meditation reduces extraneous stresses and prepares the mind for self-enquiry. We're then able to apply the teaching of Vedanta in very real and practical terms and watch as that Knowledge gradually, yet throughly, reorients our identity from one of contraction and lack to expansiveness and perpetual wholeness.

When it comes to liberation, it's really a question of "Are you *ALL IN*?"

Because if you're not all in, you're as good as out.

"May we learn to be like a river that dances and sings the songs of the Eternal, travelling and surrendering to the many bends, until she finally meets her beloved ocean."

Mundaka Upanishad

Karma Yoga and a Life of Service

In order for Vedanta to work, you really need to expose your mind to the teaching over and over again until it gradually permeates every level of the mind, heart and psyche. This does not happen overnight, but over time with sustained focus and commitment. It's not necessary (and in the vast majority of people's cases, appropriate) to completely renounce all worldly ties. It's possible to still have a family, relationships, a job and career and to still pursue liberation. It's just a little bit harder in that case to marshal your energy and focus when you have a thousand other demands, responsibilities and commitments. The key for engaging in worldly life and still pursuing enlightenment is to live life as karma yoga, which is spoken of in great detail in the Bhagavad Gita.

Karma yoga (which might be translated as "union through action") converts life to a field of service. We consecrate every action, whether grand or mundane, as a gift to God, while accepting the results of those actions, whether we deem them good or bad, as what we call *prasada*, or divine grace. Living in this way, which is to say, living for God and not for our own little ego, stokes the fires of devotion and keeps the ego in check big style. Over time, this approach to living neutralises the mind's binding attachments and aversions; both of which disturb our tranquility of mind, rendering liberation impossible.

While living a life of service and devotion, going about the world doing our dharma, or duty, we continue listening to the teaching from beginning to end, time and time again. Each time we approach it with what the Zen masters call beginner's mind;

allowing the vision of truth to unfold in our mind while working through any areas of doubt or confusion that arise with the help of our teacher.

I feel blessed to have had James as a teacher, because he has a brilliant way of making the teaching accessible and relatable to Western audiences. To be frank, Vedanta can be a dry and heady topic at the hands of some teachers, but James's humour, wit and levity made it a joy to hear. For the next few years, I travelled to attend James' seminars in Europe as often as I could, a minimum of twice a year. The great benefit of attending a seminar in person rather than self-studying at home is that, for the duration of that time away, your mind remains fixed on the topic and free of the distractions and responsibilities that would otherwise eat away at your time and focus were you at home. Without exception, any extended period spent studying Vedanta qualifies as time well spent.

Karma yoga converts life to a field of service. We consecrate every action, whether grand or mundane, as a gift to God, while accepting the results of those actions, whether we deem them good or bad, as prasada, or divine grace.

"Life is a pilgrimage. The wise man does not rest by the roadside inns. He marches direct to the domain of Eternal bliss, his ultimate destination."

Swami Sivananda

A Trip to India

At the start of 2015, I embarked on a pilgrimage to India. James was holding a three week seminar in Tiruvanamalai, the Tamil Nadu town that had been home to the adored saint Ramana Maharshi during in the first half of the twentieth century. I couldn't resist the invitation. The mere thought of India made my heart sing.

That said, I knew it was an ambitious undertaking given the constraints of my physical health. I was still struggling to function even halfway normally and required a lot of rest just to get through the day without my energy crashing. I had no question in my heart, however, that I had to do this. I knew a number of people who were going, including a dear friend, Anu, with whom I would travel, meeting up at Abu Dhabi before proceeding to Bangalore in India. It was a great expense but, with serendipitous grace, the money appeared prior to leaving courtesy of some inheritance. That was just the start of what felt like a month of continuous grace; a succession of one blessing after another.

I love travelling. While some are nervous travellers always waiting for things to go wrong, I'm like a child, wide-eyed in wonder of everything around me. I find myself mesmerised by all the different places, the airports, planes, trains and buses, all the people going about their merry way, and the ever changing scenery, views, souvenirs and cups of coffee. As long as I know where I am and where I'm meant to be, I surrender to the experience, knowing that everything is taken care of for me. I allow the activity and motion to flow through me like a river, while marvelling at the ceaseless unfoldment of it all. As it happens, I experienced the entire month in such a serendipitous state of flow. I felt like I was in complete passenger mode. I didn't have to do anything; I just watched and allowed all these wonderful sights and sounds and experiences to flow through my awareness, while filled with the joy and wonder of it all.

I landed in India with a bump, however. Upon reaching security, every passenger was interviewed by an official who wanted to know your reason for entering the country. I was honest and said that I was here to see my guru in Tamil Nadu. The official's eyes narrowed and he looked at me as though I was from another planet. I'm not so sure why that was so hard to believe for a country like India, but there you have it. He shrugged, ticked a box and let me through.

You aren't, or at least weren't at the time, allowed to bring cash into India, so whereas I would normally get some money exchanged before entering a country, I arrived empty handed. I found a cash machine, put in my card and tried to make a transaction. Declined! I had notified my bank that I would be travelling to India, but something had gone wrong on their end and the moment I tried to use my card it was blocked and cancelled. I had no money. Not even a single rupee.

If I'd been travelling alone I'm not sure what I would have done. I wouldn't have had any money to get a taxi to my hotel, which was several miles from the airport. Fortunately, I was with my friend Anu, who paid for the taxi and, when we arrived at the hotel, I made several calls to my bank before they would reactivate my card. The thought of being in a different country with no access to money was a sobering one, yet I was unperturbed because I knew that, inconvenient though it was, it was nothing that couldn't and wouldn't be sorted. Over time, that increasingly became my reaction to problems. Life, being the complex field of karma that is, is beset with challenges and problems. Even the trickiest of problems, however, come with solutions. The best we can do is to retain level headed equanimity as we reach for the appropriate solution.

I was overjoyed to be in India and felt an enormous kinship with the country and its people. I will admit that the environment was, at first, a shock to the senses, particularly for a guy who lived in a small and sleepy seaside town in the north of Scotland. I don't think the average Westerner can be quite prepared for the hectic buzz of an Indian town or city. I'll admit I was knocked for six by the sensory bombardment of constant motion, sound, sights, smells and the blazing hot sun I experienced upon arriving in Bangalore.

The roads are what I can only describe as frenetic. Travelling by car or rickshaw is, at least initially, enough to fray the nerves of the most stoic of souls, not least because of the constant cacophony of blaring horns—something only occasionally used as a warning in the West, but which serves as a kind of omnipresent courtesy call in the East. However, while there appears to be an unpredictable chaos to the roads, with lights and road signs more of a suggestion than rule, I never once witnessed an accident, so it would seem to be something of a controlled chaos. After a few days, of course, you become accustomed to the heightened pace and sensory stimulus. It simply becomes the new normal.

Whereas there's a comparatively restrained, contained feel to most Western cities, India holds nothing back. Everything is on display, loudly and unapologetically and, once you get accustomed to the heightened sensory stimulus, it's a thing of wonder. You see life in all of its uncompromising duality: things of breathtaking wonder and beauty, a joyous spirit of devotion, kindness and service that I'd never experienced in the West, as well as ugliness, decay and the tragedy of widespread poverty.

I would never want to glamorise the clear deprivation

experienced by so many even today, but I was struck that even the materially poorest of people, those with nothing but shacks by the side of the road, often appeared to have more spirit and peace in their eyes than many of the most affluent Westerners.

Indeed, I've known people with everything that money can buy with no material need unmet and yet who live wretchedly miserable lives simply because they're out of touch with the light of their own Being. When the sacred is missing from a person's life, the mind, with all of its tortuous conditioning, assumes centre stage and the result is the widespread pandemic of depression, anxiety and dysfunction we see all around us today. The person with nothing but God is infinitely richer than the person with everything but God.

I think of India as the spiritual capital of the world. Even though, as a whole, the country seems to be on course toward a more secular and materialistic trajectory—seeking to emulate the West, alas—I found South India still steeped in a rich and pervasive spirituality. Upon seeing a septic tank van garlanded with flowers and statues of Ganesha, I marvelled at how absolutely *everything* was seen as sacred, even the waste.

With shrines and temples to the various gods and goddesses of the Indian pantheon on every street corner, my eyes were greeted by symbols of the sacred just about everywhere I looked. You could clearly see that God pervaded everything, permeating the culture and the very psyche of the people even as they busily went about their worldly lives.

For Anu and I, the hotel was our sanctuary. With similar health issues, we understood and looked out for each other and were both somewhat exhausted from the travelling. The seminar venue was only a fifteen minute walk down the road, so when we weren't at classes we were back at the hotel, usually either eating or sleeping.

On occasion, I envied the more energetic and adventurous members of the group, who would take daily hikes up the sacred Mount Arunachala or go exploring the town and countryside. I had to conserve my energy, however, so I simply admired the sacred mountain from afar. This particular mountain is held as sacred in Indian mythology and is seen a literal embodiment of God. I swear you could tangibly feel it, too. The millennia of love and devotion directed at this mountain perfumed the air like sweet incense. It was, without doubt, a sacred place. Of course, all places are sacred, for everything is One, but some places you can truly feel it with your heart and soul, and Mount Arunachala is one such place.

I paid several visits to Ramanashram. It was here that Ramana Maharshi had lived out his remaining years having spent two decades in seclusion in a cave on the mountain. Ramana was celebrated throughout not just India, but the world, as a *mahatma*, or great soul. Even though his body passed away in 1950, hundreds of thousands of people still flock to his ashram each year and I could immediately tell why. As I entered the samadhi chamber, where his physical remains where interred, I was hit by a tangible wave of serenity and stillness; one so profound it nearly buckled my knees and knocked the breath from my lungs. I actually had to take a seat. The sensation lasted a good couple of minutes, but the peace and serenity I felt in its wake remained unbroken.

On the whole, I'm not a fan of crowded places. The ashram tended to get congested at peak times, but I always managed to find a place where I could sit away from the crowds and simply relax and bask in the glow of the place. I loved listening to the daily Vedic chanting, which has been performed throughout the length and breadth India in exactly the same way since time immemorial. As I listened, I could feel my mind merging into the light; the all-encompassing Awareness in which all these beauteous sights and sounds appeared in dreamlike splendour.

Each visit was special, and I'm forever glad that I made this holy pilgrimage. Though his body had been cast off six decades previously, as Ramana remarked upon his death bed, "People say I'm going away, but where can I go? I am *here*." Ramana wasn't a person, of course. He was the Self, pure Awareness illumining a body and mind. Indeed, that's what all of us are. The difference was that Ramana was fully cognisant of his true nature and, having spent two decades in deep meditation, had purified his mind to such a degree that the light shone through him in a way rare even for the enlightened.

At this point in my spiritual journey, my devotion to the teaching was beginning to bear fruit. I was resolutely clear that the key to liberation was not chasing after certain experiences or contriving high states of consciousness, but re-educating the mind with knowledge; specifically, Self-Knowledge. The real reason that we suffer isn't because we're not getting the experiences that we want. It's because the mind is operating from a paradigm of ignorance. The only way to cure ignorance is through knowledge.

The knowledge in question? "I am not this body/mind/ego entity—*I am the Awareness* in which it, and in which all form, thought and experience, arises and subsides."

Ramana knew this with every fibre of his being. That was what liberated him from worldly suffering. I knew I wasn't in India to sightsee and to accumulate experiences, memories, souvenirs and photographs. I was there to integrate and assimilate the basic teaching of Vedanta, summed up by the great saying, *Tat Twam Asi*, or "I Am That". These three words affirm our true identity as the one, all-pervading Self; the nature of which is Existence, Consciousness and limitless bliss.

Vedanta is actually quite simple. You sit and listen to the teacher as they unfold the teaching, and you then contemplate that Knowledge continuously until it gradually sinks in; until it becomes ironclad conviction. While it's not difficult to get an intellectual understanding of what's being taught, the challenging part is integrating that Knowledge deeply, thoroughly and completely into the mind, to the extent that it upgrades and overwrites your entire understanding of the nature of Self and Reality.

The way to do that is just to stick with the teaching and continually apply the process of self-enquiry to the mind—which will, until it has been tamed, will continue throwing out the same old ignorance based patterns and conditioning. It's a step by step process requiring discipline, resolve and determination. You can never afford to lose sight of the goal: specifically, freedom from the sense of limitation at the root of all existential striving and sorrow.

The solution to worldly suffering isn't to be found in the world itself. It only comes from the realisation that what we ultimately are is far more expansive, eternal and enduring than anything conceivable by the mind. Ramana Maharshi's life and legacy is a testament to that.

Above Top: Mount Arunachala, Tiruvannamalai, India.
Left: Gates to Ramanashram Right: Selfie at foot of the mountain, 2015.

When the sacred is missing from a person's life, the mind, with all of its tortuous conditioning, assumes centre stage and the result is the widespread pandemic of depression, anxiety and dysfunction we see all around us today. The person with nothing but God is infinitely richer than the person with everything but God.

"It is a confirmed fact by the Bhagavad Gita and all the Upanishads that liberation is attained by Knowledge alone."
Adi Shankaracharya

Chasing Spiritual Highs vs Seeking Knowledge

While I have no shortage of stories, there's one particular tale I'd like to share from my time in India.

My friend Anu and I met quite a few people who came to stay at our hotel (and, as it happens, the hotel staff were absolutely lovely and almost felt like family after a few weeks). I enjoyed chatting with various other guests and learning what had brought them to Tiruvanamalai. In most cases, it was a devotion to Ramana Maharshi and the desire to spend time at his ashram.

When we were asked, my friend and I would explain that we were attending a seminar by an American teacher of traditional Vedanta. Sometimes they were interested by this, but many times they were not, which was perfectly fine.

We met one particular couple who trekked into town every morning to see a *shaktipat guru;* a guru capable of transferring *shakti* or subtle energy (the Chinese call it Chi or Qi). Some yogis, after much training, are capable of harnessing the vital force and transferring it to others. It's one of those things that really has to be experienced to be believed. I first experienced it when a Qigong teacher reached out at me from across the room and I could feel the sensation of him touching me even though he was several yards away. It's possible to get a real spiritual high from the experience of shakti. You can end up feeling blissful and serene, rather like I felt when I wandered into Ramana's samadhi hall. This particular couple went for their shaktipat every morning and joked it that was better than their morning coffee.

One day, out of curiosity, they came to the Vedanta seminar. I remember James being on particularly fine, exuberant form that day as he expounded the teaching with exceptional clarity and power. One of the themes was that no experience, however exalted or sublime, can deliver liberation. Only Self-Knowledge, the knowing that we are already eternally free, whole and complete, can lead to liberation. Seeking freedom externally, in the world of form and experience, can only ever lead to further bondage. True freedom comes not from chasing pleasurable experiences, but from realising that what we truly are, pure Awareness, is already free *regardless* of the experience we're having. Whether the body is experiencing pleasure or pain and the mind peaceful or agitated, happy or sad, the Awareness that you are is absolutely fine and completely unbound, much the same way as the sun is untouched by whatever it happens to be illuminating upon the Earth.

The lady from the hotel sat next to me at the seminar, listening with full attention as James spoke, her face lit by a beaming smile. I could practically see a lightbulb igniting in her mind as she soaked in the teaching. At the break, however, it became clear that her husband was not at all open to what was being said. Although his wife was clearly inspired and open to the knowledge of Vedanta, they never attended another seminar and went back to visiting their shaktipat guru each morning for the duration of their stay.

There's nothing wrong with that, of course. Not everyone is after the same thing. That holds true in the spiritual world. Everyone is seeking liberation in a roundabout way, because we all want to be free from suffering and limitation. However, very few people are clear on what enlightenment actually is. For a great many people, enlightenment means having a different, better experience to the one they're currently having. For them, it means feeling good, getting high and experiencing exalted states of consciousness. That might entail getting hits of shakti from some guru who otherwise teaches nothing. The approach of yoga has perpetuated the notion that enlightenment is somehow about changing our experience; about making our experience different, better, or more "spiritual".

In actuality, if we're seeking freedom through an experience—be that *any* experience, including blissful, spiritual ones—we're in trouble. We're in trouble because experience constantly changes from moment to moment. There's no holding onto anything in the world of duality. Woe betide anyone who tries! The spiritual high from getting zapped with shakti is fleeting (if, in fact, you feel anything at all, because many people don't). If you're lucky it might last a day, or even a week, month or year. But it always ends, because every experience has a beginning, middle and an end. Attaching ourselves to any kind of experience as a means of freedom is ultimately futile and self-defeating. For liberation to be liberation it has to be lasting; it has to be eternal. Therefore, we can never find it from anything in this world of form, because objects and experience are, by their very nature, impermanent and fleeting.

I'm lucky to have learned this comparatively early in my life; not that it didn't take me a number of years to really grasp the lesson. If freedom is something that can be gained by *adding* something to ourselves, some experience whether gross or subtle, then we're scuppered because anything that can be gained can and, in time, will be lost again.

Only Self-Knowledge can end our existential suffering because the problem all along was one of ignorance. We suffer because we don't know who or what we are. This Self-Knowledge doesn't involve a process of addition. It's one of subtraction; of removal. We are removing the ignorance that has obscured our apprehension of our true nature.

According to the scriptures and the sages and seers over uncountable millennia, we are *already free;* right here, right now.

We were never not free.

Our problem was only ever misperception. Ignorance causes us to misinterpret reality. We see a snake where only a rope exists. Moreover, we are not only taking form and objects to be real but are investing and superimposing our sense of "I-ness", our sense of Self, onto the otherwise inert instruments of the body and mind. We take ourselves to be something we were not. When you misidentify as the body and mind, you take their limitations, pains and sorrows as yours. Through an unconscious act of false identification, you become a pained and sorrowful, suffering person.

When you come to realise the Truth of Reality, you see that you are beyond all phenomenal objects and forms. You are That in which they appear; the Light in which the whole dream of the phenomenal is apperceived.

That Light, which is *You*, is always present and always free of limitation and impurity. The freedom born of this Self-Knowledge is always yours for the taking. The only work on your part is getting the mind to truly and completely grasp this simple, yet utterly game-changing piece of Knowledge. Vedanta calls it *Raja Vidya*, the King of Knowledge. This Knowledge alone ends the quest for what was never actually lost: the light of your own true Being.

Only Self-Knowledge can end our existential suffering because the problem all along was one of ignorance. We suffer because we don't know who or what we are.

"Your true nature is limitless Consciousness. The feeling of limitation is the work of the mind."
Ramana Maharshi

Self-Realised or Certifiable?

Of course, all that I've just written, and, indeed, much of this book will, at best, make no sense to the average person. At worst, they'll think I'm some kind of deranged lunatic. I remember once asking one of my more worldly friends if he thought I was weird. He shrugged and said, "No, you just have your own ideas about things." They're not really my own ideas at all, but I'll take that.

I've found that the spiritual impulse, the prompting to go within and seek answers about the nature of the Self and Reality, is not something that can be manufactured. A person either has it or they don't. I'm tempted to say there's no "in between place", but you do get a lot of spiritually half-hearted people. Such people like to think of themselves as spiritually advanced but, when you get right down to it, rather than committing to genuine enlightenment, they're actually seeking to get something materially out of the deal. Generally, if someone is trying to use God in service of their desires, ambitions and ego, they are spiritually immature. That's not a judgement, but a simple and necessary observation.

A genuine seeker doesn't try to use God in service of their will. Instead, they align their will with God in order to serve as an instrument of dharma, or right action. As the mystic Joel S Goldsmith said, "God is not meant to glorify man. Man is meant to glorify God."

It's vital that we be very clear about our underlying motives. Are we using spiritual ideas as a salve to enhance our ego and self-concept or as a means of fulfilling our worldly desires? Or do we genuinely seek to transcend the ego and realise our inherent oneness with and non-separation from God? Only the latter can bring freedom. The former simply strengthens the chains of samsara, albeit with a pretty spiritual bow tied on top.

It can be a strangely lonely plateau when you realise that you no longer view the world in the same way as either worldly people or as most "spiritual" people do. You still understand others perfectly, of course, because you've been in their shoes and suffered all too long the relentless seesaw of pleasure and pain, desire and aversion, gain and loss that is samsara. Very few people, however, have any frame of reference for what happens when you jailbreak the mind and begin to internalise the Knowledge, "I am Awareness."

The more you sit with that Knowledge and allow it to seep into the mind, overwriting layers upon layers of ignorance and conditioning, the more the sense of being an individual, autonomous being begins to dissolve. Your "personhood" begins to diminish and you experience strange sense of transparency.

You are now aware of the ego's patterns, habitual reactions and thought processes, but far less attached to or swayed by them. You see such passing phenomena as simply waves arising in the ocean of mind, set in motion by the momentum of past actions. Your tendency to identify with mental or psychological content ceases. This conditioning will still be there to a greater or lesser degree, but it's no longer seen as "me" or "mine".

There comes a point when the person that you thought you were stands revealed as just a concept: an assumed identity; a mere conglomeration of various thought patterns, identifications and habituated desires and aversions. Try though you might, you'll never be able to find a *you* in any of it. The content of your consciousness now seems curiously impersonal to you. The false superimposition by which you projected your sense of Self, of Existence and Beingness, onto a body, mind and ego, is shattered.

Self-enquiry reveals that the only "you" that you'll ever be able to find is the pure Awareness that shines like an eternal light, present in every single experience at every single moment; always the same and ever unchanging. Losing your humanhood, you are reborn to your inherent, eternal and inalienable divinity. In essence, the wave realises that it was never separate from the vast ocean. That is the end point of the spiritual journey; the spiritual bullseye we're all aiming for.

The funny thing is, even once you cease seeing yourself as a person, that's precisely, and naturally, how others continue seeing you. It's a strange incongruity that you have no choice but to accept. After all, it's not important that others understand you, only that you understand yourself.

If you think about it, people never really encounter others in the first place. Rather, the mind creates a concept of who they *think* the other person is and that's essentially what they interact with. When you meet the meet the average human being, they essentially create an avatar of you in their mind, based, in large part, on projected ignorance and selective interpretation of information. Almost all the time, human beings see each and relate to each other through a filter of projection. Perhaps that's almost a good thing in a way, because it means that nothing in life is ever personal. How can it be, when a person isn't really seeing *you*, as you actually are, but rather a projection of their own thoughts, prejudices, conditioning and ignorance? I wasted too much energy in my earlier years trying to get others to think favourably of me. In actual fact, whether a person adores or despises you, it's not personal. How can it be? They don't know you. How can they know you when they don't even know themselves?

I find it funny that most of my friends and family haven't a clue who I am beyond the "story of Rory". I appear to possess a body and mind, of course, and I speak and present myself as a regular person. That's what everybody thinks I am because that's what everybody thinks they are. I know, however, that there's only one being in existence; one universal Consciousness illumining an entire universe of bodies and minds. It might be tempting on occasion, but I don't go shouting it out from the rooftops. Unless somebody happens to be genuinely interested in spiritual knowledge, I keep it to myself; because, really, most people don't have the capacity to understand such things.

When you've seen through the illusion and finally realised that you are the Self—pure Awareness—and not the ego, the person, you can't expect anyone else to share in that revelation. Your family, friends, colleagues and neighbours will still see you as the exact same person they've always seen. What's more, you'll probably find yourself relating to and interacting with them in the same way as before. That's because so much of what we do and say is pre-programmed and based upon the momentum of past actions and karma. It's possible that, in time, they'll notice something different about you. They might realise that you no longer stress like you once did, that you're happier and more at peace, or that you're no longer frantically chasing after objects and experiences in order to be happy.

Perhaps, some day, they may even ask about this change in you. If you tell them the truth, however, that you no longer see yourself as a person, don't expect them to understand! Unless someone has had a spiritual epiphany themselves or some grounding in Self-Knowledge, they'll probably think you've gone cuckoo. Because, let's face it, it does sound crazy. We've been hypnotised en masse to think that we are "people"; even though, if you were stop and ask somebody to point out the actual *person* they think they are, they'd be at a total loss to find it. That's because it's nowhere to be found. "Personhood" is nothing but a concept; an abstract assumption in the mind. You'll never actually be able to find this thing called a "person" because it doesn't exist outside of thought.

However, it says in the Bhagavad Gita that what the worldly view as daytime, or self-evident truth, is actually the dark night of ignorance to the Self-Realised, and vice versa. Krishna also cautions that knowers of the Self should not unsettle the minds of the worldly. In other words, don't make a show of yourself and your newfound Self-Knowledge, because it invariably won't go down too well.

"Those who think themselves free are free, and those who think themselves bound are bound. It is true that as one thinks, so one becomes."

Ashtavakra Gita

No Enlightenment Certificate

Enlightenment has nothing to do with attaining cosmic visions or enhancing the ego-self by wearing crystals, hippie clothes and diligently practising yoga, pilates and clean eating. It simply means breaking free of the delusion that you are a person; a finite, time-bound entity subject to the ravages of duality, and coming to know the boundless light of your own true nature.

It's about finding your Self—which is, admittedly, something of a joke. How could you ever *not* be your Self? What else could you be? You had to be your Self all along, or else it wouldn't be your *Self*; it would be something different entirely. It would be your not-Self.

That's pretty much the gist of the problem. As a result of maya's concealing and veiling properties, we fail to recognise what we truly are; and, groping in the twilight of ignorance, we superimpose our sense of Self onto the first objects we're aware of: our body and mind—and all of the mind's content, too. Of course, we're only ever the Self, but we get lost in delusion and take ourselves to be something other than the pure and changeless Awareness underlying our every experience.

Enlightenment is not about *adding* anything to what you are. It's about *removing* self-ignorance. Only then do you find what you never lost in the first place. You only thought it was missing because of ignorance. Once that ignorance is gone—BAM! You can't help but see everything differently even though outwardly nothing has changed.

When this Self-Knowledge finally sinks in, the desire to seek finally ends. Whereas, for many years, you may have been driven by an insatiable spiritual yearning, you now reach a point where all seeking simply ceases. That can be a little disorientating at first. But when you arrive at your destination, where else can you go? All that remains is to consolidate this liberating Knowledge and remain vigilant lest it ever get compromised. Ignorance is a slippery customer and can re-exert its hold in many, often subtle, ways. Keen vigilance always pays off in life.

Although I've used it with some frequency in this book, I don't much like the term "enlightenment". It sounds ostentatious and, much like the word "God", has been so misused over the centuries that it has lost much of its meaning. Definitions can differ so radically from person to person that it can be hard to reach any meaningful consensus on what it means.

When you realise the Self you won't think of yourself as "enlightened" anyway. Consider it a red flag if you come across somebody who goes about proclaiming themselves an "enlightened person". Enlightenment applies only to the ego, the individual, but never the Self, which is what we actually are. In fact, the Self cannot get enlightened! Why? Because there was never a time it was "endarkened." The Self *is* the Light—the self-shining Light that has no beginning and no end and which relies upon nothing else for its existence.

You might say that the ego gets enlightened, but if it is genuine liberation, then you no longer identify as the ego, so you're not going to think of yourself as having gotten enlightened.

What we truly are was never *not* enlightened. The problem was only ever ignorance; specifically, our mistaken misidentification with form and the belief that we are a body/mind/ego entity. Once that's gone, there's just *you*, and you are that which is ever free and unbound by anything in the phenomenal world.

Suffering and limitation, old age, sickness and death clearly affect the body and the mind. They don't, however, affect the boundless field of Awareness in which the body and mind are experienced. At the relative level, the person you appear to be will continue to experience the ups and downs of duality because just that's the way the game of form works.

But the real you will always be untouched by even the worst of what this world can throw at you. Nothing affects the light of Awareness. It shines irrespective of whatever is happening within it. The Self shines eternally, without beginning and end; outliving the births and deaths of all the stars, galaxies and universes.

Again, the great thing is that you don't need to do *anything* to "become" this Self. It's what you already are and always have been. All that's necessary is to reeducate the mind and keep ignorance from creeping back in.

Once you've found the teaching and a qualified teacher, the journey to liberation is, in large part, just a matter of putting in the necessary time, effort and focus. Instead of losing yourself in worldly concerns, of which there are countless in what Taoism calls "the world of the ten thousand things", what you need to do is to constantly redirect your mind and heart back to the basic Truth, "I am Awareness". Old habits and thought patterns die hard. It may take considerable time and effort until you reach the tipping point and the Self-Knowledge fully sinks in.

It's possible you may experience epiphanies along the way; moments in which the ties of the mind loosen and your perception of Reality shifts, enabling you to taste the limitlessness, wonder and bliss of your own nature. I've documented a couple of such epiphanies here. They may last weeks, months or years—or, more likely, mere minutes. The mind eagerly tends to reassert itself, dragging you back to your worldly attachments and concerns. What these epiphanies provide, however, is a taste of freedom. You get a glimpse of what life can be when you're no longer pulled under by the waves of samsara and entangled by all of the mind's binding attachments, addictions, desires and fears.

If you process such an experience correctly, it ought give you the sense that your joy does not come from outer circumstances, but from deep within your own Self. This will increase your value for Self-Realisation and bolster your motivation and determination to, in the words of the Bible, "Fight the good fight, finish the course and keep the faith."

When liberation comes you may not even notice it at first. It's not an event as such. The ground doesn't suddenly shake and rays of light shoot down from heaven, although it would be cool if they did. You won't receive a certificate in the mail to say that you've graduated and got first class honours in enlightenment. Again, that would be neat, but you'll be waiting a long time for it.

I experienced it as something that snuck up on me over time. I came to notice that my outlook and reaction to life had fundamentally shifted. My spiritual seeking had resolutely ended and so, too, did my worldly seeking. I ceased desiring things. Oh, sure, I might get a desire for things like chocolate, coffee and listening to my favourite music or whatever. I still experience likes and dislikes, but they generally rank as low-grade and non-binding. It was the biggies that faded away: the desire to attain things that I thought would make me feel whole, complete and happy.

Over time, I developed a sense of what I'd describe as inner sufficiency; the knowing that I didn't need anything external in order to be happy. I found I was just happy in myself. Not that I'd go about with a constant grin on my face. Unless I've perhaps had a couple of glasses of wine, I don't think I'm a terribly effusive guy, so I wasn't running about jumping for joy. But I had an inner contentment and satisfaction. I became content with simplicity, with minimalism and with simply having what I had. I already had a great love of nature, but this came into sharper focus. Whereas some express their devotion in temples and churches, I tend to see God most clearly in the natural world, far from anything man-made. I find joy in the simplest of things, such as looking at a flower or tree or gazing up at the sky in wonder.

The need for striving and struggle disappeared. I no longer wanted anything I didn't have. I lost any trace of ambition. I know that everything I need is provided by God; I trust that and have found it to be very much the case. This is something that will not likely be appreciated by worldly people. In fact, I've been attacked for it, and judged and shamed for of my lack of ambition.

Fortunately, another of the great things about freedom is that you no longer care much what others think. That's a huge breakthrough for someone who spent the early part of his life caring all together too much about the tyranny of other peoples' opinions.

I'm careful who I say this to, but I no longer see myself as a person. "Rory" is just a helpful concept that makes worldly interaction easy; a label slapped upon a body and a conglomeration of thoughts, habits, personality type, memories and values. The person is kind of like an avatar that allows Consciousness to function in this Virtual Reality-type world.

I'd long been at battle with this poor guy I thought I was; ruthlessly self critical and prone to fixating on every last perceived flaw. For whatever reason, I'd found it easy to see the light in others, but not in myself. How funny is that. I learned that the only appropriate way to relate to this part of ourselves, our avatar, is love. It can be a long process, however, learning to rewire a lifelong negative self-image and deeply ingrained thought processes. It takes as long as it takes, and that is fine.

Love is the only appropriate response to life. We can love it all, including our own ego pseudo-self, with all of its strengths and weaknesses, its victories and failings, virtues and foibles. It's all God; all divine.

Self-Knowledge yields the realisation that we, ourselves, don't actually *do* anything anyway. The phenomenal realm, as experienced by the mind and senses, is a kaleidoscopic flow of patterning determined by factors far outside our control. This grand game of life is run by Ishvara, or God, and we, as the Awareness in which it all appears, simply witness it. It ebbs and flows, directed by the momentum of past karma. While the body and mind are part of the creation and are subject to its laws, as the Self, we are unaffected and untouched by any of it. We are simply the witness; all-pervading like the sky and ever-shining like the sun.

It all just happens *in* us. Everything comes and goes, and it's all fine because we, ourselves, are like space. We neither come nor go. We just *are*; more eternal than time and space itself.

Our only problem is when we forget that and get pulled back into identification with form. This will, most likely, happen for quite some time even after Self-Realisation. It might almost feel as though some invisible force is pressing the "on" and "off" switch.

The steady contemplation of our nature as Awareness is called nididhyasana in Vedantic terminology. It's been said that for every hour we spend in the first stage of Vedanta, listening to the teaching, we should then spend a hundred hours going over the reasoning in our head and a thousand hours meditating upon it deeply and with great focus and clarity.

So, for all there's nothing we can do to become the Self—because we're already the Self and cannot be anything else—it does take considerable effort to reorient and retrain the mind. As I learned the hard way, the mind can be our greatest friend or our most implacable and merciless foe. We alone decide which. An untamed mind is the root of enormous suffering and chaos. On the other hand, a cultivated and refined mind is an instrument for liberation. A sufficiently purified mind allows our true light to radiate from us and to bless all whom we meet. What a gift to offer the world. But, once again, it takes time, perseverance and grit. As the saying goes, everything is difficult before it gets easy.

I made a number of missteps as I practised nididhyasana over the next few years post-India. I got suckered by my psychological blind spots and ended up down one or two avenues that weren't in line with who I was and who I was meant to be. I assumed that I was "finished" before I truly was and I relaxed my efforts, only to be in for a fright when samsara again managed to get its hooks into me. Life likes to test us. The moment you think, "That's it, I've done it," you can pretty much bet that God is thinking, "Oh, *really*—have you now...?"

There was no lasting damage in my case, but I learned the supreme importance of vigilance and humility. In time to come, my body and mind would be put through the fire big style. That, as it happens, would actually be immensely purifying, allowing my Self-Knowledge to cement in leaps and bounds. The true alchemy of living involves accepting and embracing all of life's challenges and adversities and using them as grist for the mill of self-enquiry.

Here's a helpful thought which I very much believe to be true. All of life is secretly conspiring to awaken us from the dream of separation into full realisation of the divine unity of all things.

In spite of how it might often seem, this is not a cruel reality. It's a cosmic game of hide and seek. The hurt and pain is not there to torment you. It's there to jolt you awake; compelling you to remember the vastness of what you truly are, emboldening you to claim your divine birthright.

"The sage battles his own ego; the fool battles everyone else's."

Sufi proverb

Some Spiritual Misconceptions

Along my journey, I encountered a mountain of misconceptions about enlightenment—some of which were actually great impediments to any kind of legitimate spiritual progress.

One, prevalent in New Age circles, is the notion that enlightenment is something called "ascension", in which our entire being, physical body and all, somehow transmutes into pure energy. It's usually accompanied by the narrative that the entire world is moving out of duality into a state of Oneness (a kind of "collective ascension", if you will). These ideas are born of confusion about the nature of reality. They stem from the belief that duality is real and that, in order to get out of it, we have to somehow transform duality into Non-duality. That's like trying to perfect a shadow into substance. Try though you might, it's never going to happen, because it can't.

Part of the problem is that virtually all spiritual teachings are inherently dualistic, even if they pay lip service to Non-duality. The idea that we are a "lower self" that must ascend into a "Higher Self" is one of the greatest fallacies in the spiritual scene.

There is no lower self. There's only ONE SELF and we already are it. What else could we be? Our problem is not that we're a lower self that has yet to merge into a higher state of consciousness. The problem is that we've fallen under the spell of ignorance, maya, and we're identifying with name and form. By mistakingly assuming that we're the body/mind/ego, we superimpose a raft of painful limitations upon ourselves. We cast ourselves as a person, a limited entity subject to birth, ageing, death and all manner of sorrows, struggles and fleeting joys in between. That's the only "lower self" and it's nothing but a case of false superimposition. Through ignorance, we're superimposing the sense of "I" or "I am-ness", which belongs to the Self, onto form; onto objects of gross and subtle perception.

What we are is the boundless space of Awareness in which this entire world (and the body and mind and all of its fantasies and fears, desires and attachments) is experienced. The poor little lower self is only a false idea we have about ourselves. We do not overcome this false self by trying to transform it into something real and lasting. We simply recognise the ignorance for what it is and turn our mind to what we truly are: whole, complete and limitless by nature.

The scriptures make it clear that the Self is unborn and what is unborn can never die. It knows no limitation because limitation necessitates finitude. We can never *not* be whole. Only false thinking can make it seem otherwise.

We don't have to go anywhere to become whole. We don't have to get to "the other shore", because there is no other shore. We're already there. This Awareness, which is our true essence, is without limit, so there's nothing and nowhere it is not. Certainly, these bodies and minds are great little vehicles for helping us function in the world and take part in the divine "sport" of maya. But they are just instruments reflecting the light of our Consciousness much as the moon reflects the light of the sun.

Luckily for me, I eventually got free of the erroneous idea that enlightenment is about "perfecting" the self. There is no perfecting the body and mind. They are products of maya and, as such, will always be subject to duality. The key to ending suffering is the realisation that this doesn't matter, because we are neither the body or mind. We are something infinitely greater and more expansive; the Existence, Consciousness and Bliss that is the Self. Again, we don't have to do anything to *become* that Self. It's already a fully accomplished fact. All we need to do is to re-educate our mind until it finally gets the message.

Whereas some spiritual teachings purport enlightenment to be some kind of godlike state replete with superpowers, in actual fact, it's simply a reorientation of the mind accomplished by the removal of ignorance. You won't suddenly be able to walk on water and raise the dead. Your bank account won't magically be full, people won't be falling over you in worship as you walk the streets and your worldly problems won't suddenly disappear (although they may well seem a whole lot less relevant and stressful to you).

The reality is subtler, yet no less wonderful. You'll feel happy and complete in yourself. You'll experience a steady sense of satisfactoriness with life even if it's not all a bed of roses.

I long laboured under the delusion that getting to the end of the spiritual path would somehow transform everything in my life. In actuality, our outer life remains the same as it was before. What changes is the way we see it all.

To quote the words of T.S. Elliot:

"The end of all our exploring will be to arrive where we started and know the place for the first time."

Nothing changes, yet, at the same time, everything changes, because the world is now stripped of its frightening "realness". You begin to see it all as just the play of light; as shadows dancing upon the cave wall, to borrow Plato's famous cave allegory. The world goes on just as it did before, and you haven't gained anything outwardly by your spiritual pursuits. At the same time, by re-contextualising your entire understanding of yourself and reality you find you have attained the most important thing imaginable: liberation from suffering.

You no longer seek happiness in an unreal world. Why would

you when you've finally discovered a ceaseless well of wholeness in your own Self? The Kingdom of God is within; and its location is your own, ever present, eternally available Consciousness. When you come to realise that everything is God, and that you are That, what can you do but live your days in a perpetual state of wonder, fulfilment and joy? That's the real ascension: an ascension in our level of understanding and Knowledge, and it really is the coolest thing imaginable.

We don't have to go anywhere to become whole. We don't have to get to "the other shore", because there is no other shore. We're already there. This Awareness, which is our true essence, is without limit, so there's nothing and nowhere it is not.

"Let the waves of the universe rise and fall as they will. You have nothing to gain or lose. You are the ocean."

Ashtavakra Gita

Nothing to Get From the World

So, how do you relate to the world once your sense of identification shifts from the limited body/mind/ego to unbound Awareness?

First of all, it's worth reiterating that it usually takes considerable time for Self-Knowledge to become fully integrated into all levels of the mind, heart and psyche. As any honest spiritual seeker will attest, it's not uncommon in deep meditation or contemplation to find yourself swept up by grand epiphanies in which you experience your oneness and unity with the Eternal, only to find yourself quickly pulled back into identification with the body, mind and the various problems of daily living.

This flipping "on" and "off" may continue for some years. You may well taste the expansiveness and freedom of your true nature as you continue with your study and practice, only to find the gravity of the mind's conditioning pulling you back into samsara. It definitely takes time and consistent effort to fully re-orient the mind to a new default. It is, however, most certainly worth the time and effort.

One of the surest signs of progress is when all seeking simply vanishes; both material and spiritual seeking. That's when I knew I'd gotten to the end of my spiritual search. The need to keep seeking just dissipated as I realised, "Heck, this is it. There's nowhere else to go, is there?"

When you come to realise that the Self is everything everywhere at all times, the need to go any place else disappears. It's already here, and I am It, so where is there to go and what is there to become? It's all already attained, now. The need to seek anything at all ends when we realise that, like the absent-minded professor searching for the hat sitting atop his head the entire time, we already had and were all that we were seeking.

The end of seeking might initially feel strange and disorientating, particularly if your spiritual quest had been such a large and consuming part of your life. All of a sudden, that imperative, that deep seated need, is no longer there and you are left with just your Self and the dawning realisation that everything is actually quite perfect exactly as it is, for it is all God.

The blossoming of this Self-Knowledge brings inner changes aplenty, although I found that I had gained nothing tangible outwardly. Fortunately, by that point, I was fine with that because I wasn't looking to *get* anything from the endeavour. I didn't want God's things; I wanted God.

To others at least, I was exactly the same Rory. My life situation remained unchanged. Whereas most people spend their first few decades of life engaging with the material world and establishing careers and families, mine had become largely a kind of hermit existence, precipitated by health limitations and directed by my yearning to be spiritually free.

I realised I'd finally gotten what I wanted when the need to keep pursuing liberation ceased. I found myself struck by the simple yet earth-shattering realisation, *"This is it!"* Where else was there to go? Why keep chasing my Self when, in reality, it was never not present? After all, if I'm not here, right now, then I'm not anywhere!

All those years of seeking and striving, of study and meditation, only to realise that what I was looking for, my Self, *was always here all along,* never separate from me and closer to me than my own breath. I'd found what I'd never lost. It almost seems like a cosmic joke when we realise that we already *have* and *are* everything we were ever looking for!

Some teachings claim that the world "disappears" upon Self-Realisation. That's not true. It only disappears in the sense that you no longer see it as inherently real and separate from yourself. When you realise who you are, the phenomenal universe continues doing its thing as it has and will continue to do until the eventual dissolution of the entire cosmos.

The Self-Realised person will remain in their body until their prarabdha karma (the karma apportioned to play out in this lifetime) has been exhausted; not before, and not after. For the one who knows the Self, what changes is not the world itself, but our relationship with it.

Most people spend their lives chasing the things they think will bring lasting happiness and fulfilment. When we realise, however, that true and sustained satisfaction and fulfilment are nowhere to found in the world, but only in ourselves, there's no longer anything for us to seek, acquire and get in the world. We already have it all. We derive our sense of wholeness and completeness from within, from knowing and tasting the limitlessness of our true nature, independently of whatever may be happening in the world of form.

What a wonderful, blessed relief that is! Contrary to popular belief, the world does *not* need to be a certain way in order for us to be happy. While we still have our own set of likes and dislikes, these are converted to optional preferences rather than driving demands that we place upon life and other people.

Instead of focusing on what we can get from the world, we begin focusing on what we can give to the world. Our relationship to life becomes contributory rather than extractive.

That in itself is an enormous evolutionary breakthrough. We live in a highly materialistic and ego driven culture which deliberately targets, heightens and weaponises the human sense of lack and insufficiency. Not only that, but it actively cultivates greed and avarice, hypnotising us to believe that acquiring objects and experiences is the way to satiate our inner hunger—which, as it happens, is always a misdirected spiritual hunger.

When that hunger is no longer there, and as long we have a roof over our head and food in our belly, what is there left to get? Life is no longer an exercise in getting, but in giving.

Part 3

DHARMA, DUTY AND FREEDOM AMID ADVERSITY

"I slept and dreamt that life was joy. I awoke and saw that life was duty. I acted and, behold, duty was joy."

Rabindranath Tagore

We Each Have a Dharma to Fulfil

This next section marks a shift from the spiritual to the more mundane; from the impersonal Eternal Self to the time-bound individual self. As such, it may disappoint some, but it's a necessary transition. For even once we've seen through the illusion of being a finite entity inhabiting a separate material world, we still have to—as the Zen Masters say, "chop wood and carry water". For the vast majority of us, it's neither appropriate nor necessary to go live in a cave for the rest of our lives. Instead, we simply get on with our lives as set up by the momentum of our past karma.

As long as we're in this world we are here to contribute to it; to play our part and offer something back in service of the totality. God, or That which is the very essence and substance of the creation, gives of Itself freely, providing us with a body and mind and enough to sustain us materially for an entire lifetime. In return, it's only appropriate that we offer up our lives in service of God. We do this by following our dharma with impeccable resolve.

The Vedas, of which Vedanta is the crown jewel, make it clear that we each have a dharma to fulfil; a particular service that we were born to offer the world.

Many people these days struggle to find their their path and purpose in life. It's actually pretty simple, however, because it's already pre-installed within us *as* our innermost nature. Depending upon our nature, we may be a natural spiritual adept, or someone suited to a position of leadership, a teacher or educator, an artist, communicator, visionary or innovator. We might be somebody whose warrior spirit impels us to stand up and fight for justice and order. Or perhaps our skills lie in business and finance, or suited to the service industry in some way. While some jobs tend to be seen as more prestigious and important than others, each are ultimately essential to the smooth functioning of society. We each hold a different piece of the cosmic jigsaw.

Our path through life is determined by our inherent nature and our natural talents, skills and interests. Of course, there's infinitely much more to our lives than the jobs that we do, but the key point is that we all have a dharma; a duty that is not self-chosen, but is bestowed upon us by virtue of our karma and the very composition of our subtle body (mind, intellect and ego).

Without question, I knew from a young age that I was a writer and creator. That's what I was made to be. By the time I was five years old, I spent a fair bit of my time alone crafting stories, adventures and fantasy lands drawn from the rich wellspring of my imagination. I remember being on holiday in Wales when I was around six and being upset that I hadn't brought paper—and there wasn't a scrap of it in the apartment we were staying in. I was so desperate to draw and write that I began using plastic shopping bags in lieu of paper. My parents duly took the hint and bought me a sketchpad, and I was as content as could be.

As I grew up, I knew I didn't just want to create, however. I wanted to use my work not only to entertain, but to help people. I had a deep and driving desire to change the world in some small way. By the time I reached my late teens, I realised that I could combine my creative work with the spiritual knowledge now guiding and illuminating my life.

It would be easy for a cynic to dismiss that as pompous or conceited, but my intent was pure. I didn't want to work for fame, fortune or self aggrandisement. Painfully aware of the universality of human suffering, I wanted to use words and stories to help open people's eyes to a deeper aspect of Reality; to that which is beyond the world of the senses and shining in the hearts of all beings. I wanted to show people how beautiful they truly were. That was the target, and words were my arrows. As to how good my aim was, that's another story.

"A writer's life and work are not a gift to mankind; they are its necessity."

Toni Morrison

A Writer's Story

I was born a writer. Believe it or not, I came up with an idea for a novel or series of novels when I was only five or six years old. At the core of my mind, heart and imagination lay this rich inner realm; a place of worlds within worlds, ancient civilisations, races that only I knew, as well as all kinds of characters, heroes, villains and adventures.

Ten years passed and, aged sixteen, I finally committed to sharing this inner world with others. With a folder full of notes, drawings, maps and charts, all of which I still have, I began developing the ideas and mapping out the plot, characters and themes. I'd long been compelled by the endless possibilities of fantasy and science-fiction. Relishing the freedom of creating my own universe with its own set of rules, I set about merging these genres with an underlying spiritual message. It wasn't until comparatively recently that I learned there was a technical term for such work: visionary fiction, although it's not a genre many are familiar with.

I poured my heart and soul into what became "The Key of Alanar", the book of which I'm probably the most proud. Alas, I failed to find a publisher, so I set it aside and wrote another book, designed as a second entry point to what had been envisaged as a multi-volume series. I began to feel that "The Key of Alanar" might have been a little esoteric and uncompromising for some, featuring a complex protagonist who falls from the path of his own dharma and becomes lured into dark and dangerous anti-hero territory. It's actually the most authentic story I could tell, for, as I was learning, it's often the pain, adversity and our seeming mistakes in life that compel to awaken to who and what we truly are.

My second novel, "Eladria", featured a more straightforward protagonist: a fiery, headstrong and determined teenage princess-turned-fugitive. It was also ultimately also a story about enlightenment, but designed as a breezier read. This time, I did find a publisher and the book was released in the Summer of 2013.

I'd figured that the hard part of writing a book was the actual writing of it. I was wrong! The hard part, unless you happen to have a recognisable name, brand and a large enough platform, is actually convincing people to buy and read your book. My publisher was a then brand new imprint of a larger company, and I didn't get much, if any, support in the promotion side of things. I tried as best I could, but the release came and went, and after an initial flurry of sales and highly encouraging reviews, the book sank without trace.

Undeterred, I rewrote "The Key of Alanar" for probably the tenth time until I was finally satisfied with it and I published it myself two years later. I had no expectations by this point and basically saw it as a gift to the world. Alas, however, in spite of the love, time and devotion I put into crafting the best book I could possibly write, "The Key of Alanar" didn't make so much as a ripple. It didn't help that, by this point, self-publishing had saturated the market, particularly when it came to fiction. What's more, I'm very clear that my dharma does *not* lie in sales. I considered giving away the book for free, simply because I wanted to share its message and a deeper vision of reality. The sobering reality, however, is that even if you give away your work for free, due to the sheer volume of material out there, it's unlikely anyone will ever bother to download much less read it.

By this point, between 2015 and 2017, I was deeply committed to Vedanta endeavouring to live my life as a karma yogi. That meant fulfilling my dharma, consecrating my actions as service to God, and taking the results of those actions as divine providence, whether seemingly fortuitous or not. That, according to Vedanta, is the best way to navigate this world without becoming stressed to high heaven and without reinforcing the ego's entrenched and manifold desires, attachments and aversions.

I felt with the entirety of my being that I was here to communicate: to write, to share stories, ideas and knowledge that would help others navigate this world and reach for something greater—not outside of them in other people, experiences, things and acquisitions, but inside of them at the shining core of their being. Could it be that I was working too indirectly?

My initial hope, as youthfully idealistic as it was, had been to use fiction as a way of sharing spiritual knowledge. I thought that if I could open people's minds to new ways of thinking and perceiving reality, I could change lives and switch them onto something greater. I didn't realise that there was little to no market for what I was creating. It transpired that the average genre reader was not looking for—and was, in many cases, actively averse to—themes of a spiritual nature. In my earnest naivety, I'd set out to enlighten the world. A noble endeavour, perhaps, but also something of a fool's errand.

I changed tack, figuring that perhaps it would be better to share spiritual knowledge with those that actually wanted it. A radical notion, huh? It actually did feel radical for me at the time. After all, who was *I* to write spiritual books? I had enormous confidence in the knowledge itself, but not so much in myself as an instrument of that knowledge.

Nevertheless, I kept my head down and carried on writing. I created a blog in which I shared reflections on my spiritual path and topics such as meditation, Self-Realisation, enlightenment and daily living. I only had about four or five readers, although it's a wonder I had any at all, because I never promoted it and I was still honing my writing skills. That said, it didn't really matter to me that I had almost no audience. Writing was just something I had to do. The more I wrote, the better I got at it. Like many things in life, it's obviously not something you're born good at. A skill like any other, it can take years to find, develop and refine your writing style.

My first spiritual book began as an attempt to decipher the Tao Te Ching. I'd been fascinated by this ancient text from the moment I first picked up a copy, even though the verses could be cryptic and, quite frankly, incomprehensible. I decided to take a chapter a day and, using multiple translations as my blueprint, set out to compile a version that offered clarity and ease of reading while retaining, I believe, the essence of the teaching. I wrote a commentary to each chapter, sharing my own interpretation and exploring some of the key themes.

At first, my only ambition to publish was simply to post a chapter a day on a new blog I created titled "Daily Tao". Again, I didn't promote it. I just allowed people to find it themselves. I trusted that anyone who was meant to read it would end up doing so. That, as it happens, has been my philosophy ever since. I offer myself as a channel, allowing the words to flow through me, and then I hand it over to the Source of all creativity, letting Ishvara, or God, be both my agent and publicist. That may not always be an expedient process, but over time, I found more and more people gravitating to my work and expressing gratitude and appreciation for it. Although I certainly wasn't doing it for praise and adulation, the encouragement motivated me to keep on writing.

Before long, I created another blog, "Beyond the Dream", inspired by all that I was learning from Vedanta. I had the idea that I could somehow distil the essence of the teaching in a simplified way that might have a wider reach than just Vedanta students.

It was a noble endeavour and, at times, I maybe succeeded. I came to realise, however, that Vedanta is an advanced and specialised teaching not intended for a general audience. It's university level spiritual knowledge for people that are really, truly serious about graduating. While many modern teachers cherry pick the highlights of Vedanta and repackage it as their own teaching, I came to realise that Vedanta's power lay in its completeness and comprehensiveness. Far from a selection of inspirational sound bytes, Vedanta is a system; a body of knowledge that must be respected and protected. As I'd learned from my own experience, it's not enough to simply tell someone they are the Self; you actually have to prove it to them, and Vedanta is uniquely tooled to do just that. At any rate, my commitment to Vedanta and my dharma as a writer and communicator was about to come together in a most serendipitous marriage.

Proud author of two spiritual fantasy/sci-fi novels, "Eladria" (2013) and "The Key of Alanar" (2015).

"Our body and mind function in the world of time, but the roots of our being are in Eternity."

Hari Prasad Shastri

A Dream and a Question

I harboured no real ambition to become a Vedanta teacher; even though I knew, strangely reluctantly at first, that teaching was part of my dharma. The thing is, however, I'd never much liked being in the spotlight. I found myself quite content studying in private, immersing myself in the scriptures and, most crucially, applying the Knowledge to my mind. That, as it happens, is the key to success and also the greatest challenge a seeker can face, for ignorance is nothing if not a relentless adversary.

Over time, I began experiencing the fruits of Self-Knowledge and my impetus to seek fell away of its own accord. However, even when I realised that my spiritual quest was over, my love of and dedication to Vedanta remained. I still wasn't ready to teach, but I continued writing my blog and that seemed quite sufficient for a few years. It transpires, however, that Ishvara, as Controller of the creation, decided that I was capable of more. I was to be given a choice.

One night, I experienced a vivid dream in which I found myself back at my old high school. My guru, James, appeared and I greeted him with love as we chatted in one of the corridors, students busily flitting around us. I only dream about James on occasion. When I do, I usually come away with the sense that the dream had some deeper symbolic meaning. It's only now, while writing this, that I realise the setting, my school, was highly appropriate as a meeting place for my teacher. But, then, this particular dream was far less cryptic and more literal than the majority of my dreams.

Pointedly and without pretence, James asked me what I wanted to do with my life; specifically what I, as a writer, wanted *write* about.

"I want to write about the Self," I responded without the slightest hesitation or doubt. "I want to write about God; about Truth."

In that moment, it seemed I'd made a commitment and I had done so with laser-like focus and crystal clear intent. Clearly pleased by my decision, James's face lit up with a wonderful, radiant smile and he gave me a warm and loving hug. Everything faded and I don't remember anything more, but the exchange remained with me ever since and I can still picture the scene so vividly.

In the back of my mind, I'd been thinking about writing a book on the Bhagavad Gita, much as I had with the Tao Te Ching. The Gita seemed like an altogether more ambitious project, and I wasn't entirely sure that I could do it justice. Until, that was, I remembered that "I" never do anything to begin with. Like all artists and creative beings, whether they consciously realise it or not, I was simply the conduit. The work is never done by me; it's done through me. I believe that's what Jesus was talking about when he said:

"The words that I have spoken to you do not come from me.
The Father, who dwells in me, doeth the works."

With that in mind, I set to work. I read and took copious notes from some ten thousand pages worth of translations by Adi Shankaracharya, Swami Chinmayananda, Swami Dayananda and Swami Paramarthananda; all teachers from my lineage. I listened to audio seminars by James, Swami Paramarthananda and other teachers. I played recitations of the verses in Sanskrit over and over as I worked on each chapter.

It so transpires that my degree in Social Science had trained me to gather, evaluate and present complex information in a clear and easily digestible manner. That, and years of training myself as a writer, had prepared me well for the endeavour. It was only a matter of showing up at the page and putting it all together. It took over a year, but I ended up with not only an accessible and hopefully clear translation of the text, but also a comprehensive commentary which distilled the core of Vedantic teaching into a single volume.

The interesting part was that, after sending the first few chapters to James, he and Sundari invited me to teach Vedanta as one of Shining World's endorsed teachers. Although aware of the tremendous responsibility that entailed, I agreed. It felt right; as though something had suddenly clicked into place.

I'd finally realised what I was here to do at an outer level. It had taken almost forty years to get to that point, but I could now see my dharma; the way in which my jiva, my personal self, was tooled to contribute to the world. Until that point, nothing along my life's path had been quite hit the spot. For so many years, I'd been fumbling around, trying so very hard to make my life "work"; and my seeming inability to get anywhere had been a source of frustration and confusion.

Looking back now, I can see how absolutely everything—every experience and undertaking, every seeming failure and dead end—had lead me and prepared me for where I was meant to be. Life has a funny way of doing that. Each step of our way is divinely guided, including our so perceived missteps. When looked at from a higher vantage point, there are no missteps. It's all God and everything is leading us back to the realisation that we were never and can never be separate from God.

In a sense, life is one grand conspiracy. Unlike the many neurotic, manmade conspiracy theories circling the drain, here's a conspiracy theory worth paying heed to, for it's the only one capable of freeing the mind. The gist of it? Life is One—one Divine substance and Intelligence and, believe it or not, everything that happens in life is conspiring to awaken you to that supremely liberating realisation of Unity and non-separation.

If I have any purpose at all in writing this book, it's simply to get you in on this grand conspiracy and help you to see that you are God, whether you like it or not!

A true labour of love; "Bhagavad Gita - The Divine Song" was released in 2019.

"It is within my power either to serve God or not to serve Him. Serving Him, I add to my own good and the good of the whole world. Not serving Him, I forfeit my own good and deprive the world of that good, which was in my power to create."

Leo Tolstoy

The Teacher is a Mirror

Rome wasn't built in a day and, unless you happen to be a highly qualified seeker, it's unlikely the spiritual path will bring you to your destination overnight (although the paradox is, of course, that you were never at any point *not* at your destination, but that's another story).

It had taken me years to get the spiritual thing sussed; to figure out who I was and what, at the relative level, I was meant to do in the world. I'd long had the desire to help others and, having finally tasted the liberation of knowing myself as Awareness, I naturally felt compelled to share what I'd learned. Although I'm far from the world authority on Vedanta, I am a good communicator and was only too happy to share my knowledge and experience.

I believe that such a desire to share comes from a place of compassion. When you find something that helps you at a profound level, it's natural to want to share it with others. The obvious way of doing so is to share the knowledge that's been gifted to you. That said, it's not everybody's dharma to be a teacher. Which is maybe just as well, because assuming the role of teacher can prove irresistibly tantalising to the ego.

Sadly, the spiritual arena can be a minefield when it comes to false teachers; self-aggrandising gurus whose egos have totally circumvented their Self-Knowledge and are using it, whether consciously or unconsciously, to bolster their own image, power and bank balance.

A true teacher simply wants to help others. They don't care about the number of followers they have or how many people attend their seminars. Ideally, they won't be using their followers to make a quick buck, either. A genuine teacher avoids false promises and appealing to people's egos by promising they can attain all of their desires and goals.

In fact, a true teacher will reveal to the student the part of them that's beyond desire; the part that is always and ever whole, complete and at peace, even amid the push and pull of material living. They have but one objective: not even revealing the Self, because the Self, being self-shining and self-revealing, does that all by itself—but to remove self-ignorance about the nature of that Self. Nothing more, nothing less. When the false is removed, what remains is Truth.

That was my only desire as I began corresponding with Vedanta students from around the world, helping support them on their journey and answering questions and doubts as best I could. As I embraced this new dharma, I made the acquaintance of and friendship with a number truly beautiful people whose light shines with remarkable purity and grace.

While it's true that not everyone is a suitable candidate for Vedanta, it's rare that I've had to turn anyone away, and where appropriate I try to help to the best of my capacity. Vedanta students tend to be mature, refined and gracious individuals. They just want to know the truth, with no agendas and no underlying motivations other than the desire for freedom. That's why, if so asked, I do what I can to help.

It's especially satisfying working with advanced souls who are truly committed to Self-Realisation and who have the necessary drive, motivation and, perhaps most importantly, purity of mind, to succeed. When the mental qualifications are in place, they may simply need a gentle push or the resolution of a minor doubt or misunderstanding—and they've got it! It's an absolute joy to see someone take flight as they reclaim their birthright as pure, simple, ever present Awareness.

Of course, not everybody "gets it". You really have to be *ready* to get it. The results are, as with all things, determined by karma. It's fine with me either way, because when a person seeks my assistance, I already see them as pure, whole and complete irrespective of how they see themselves. That, I believe, is one of the greatest gifts we can give another being. Instead of focusing on the superficial levels of personality and conditioning, including their words and behaviour, we see them for what they truly are at the core of their being.

When you find yourself in the public eye in any capacity, however large or small, it can be interesting seeing how people react to you. No matter who you are and what you're doing, people's reactions to you will likely run the full gamut from adoration to hatred. It doesn't really matter either, because it's all more or less projection. That's the way the human mind works. I've found that people are inclined to offer love and praise when you're telling them what they want to hear. Quite often, however, particularly with more psychologically needy people, the moment you say what they don't want to hear, or fail to do something they want you to do, that love can turn to anger or disdain with startling rapidity.

Such is the nature of life. As long as you live a dharmic life and do your best to help people and respond appropriately to each situation, what others think of you is immaterial. Nothing anybody does or says can affect Awareness. Nothing in this world can touch it, for no shadows can fall upon the sun.

I have found that some spiritual seekers have an unfortunate tendency to place more emphasis on the teacher than the actual teaching. Some teachers may actively encourage this if they are looking to inflate their own ego. While Indian tradition holds the guru as a living embodiment of God (which *all* beings ultimately are, of course), it's my opinion that, in the modern age, a teacher should be seen simply as a guide and friend. They're not there to be worshipped; they are there to worship God by sharing Truth, and nothing more. If you encounter a teacher who wants you to worship them, please—run for the hills!

The subject matter of Vedanta is nothing but the Self; You. The rest is window dressing. The guru serves as a mirror, and their job is to reveal to you your own Self.

Serving as a mirror can come with some unwanted effects, of course. The teacher obviously holds a position of authority and this can elicit psychological transference from students. As a result, some students may think they are in love with you or, if you are a certain age, are liable to transfer unresolved parental issues onto you (in other words, they want you to adopt a "father" or "mother" role for them, and if they have issues with their own parents they may even unconsciously project those onto you). This is obviously am impediment in the student-teacher relationship as it diverts focus from the teaching.

Again, this position of power can be kryptonite to the teacher who hasn't yet resolved certain psychological issues or proclivities and "kept the house clean", so to speak.

Students must always be vigilant and discerning. The power dynamic inherent in teaching has an unfortunate tendency to attract attention-hungry narcissists. Beset with glib charm, these predators often manage to build substantial followings, which are then preyed upon as they seek to satisfy whatever sexual or monetary desires might be prevalent. Aside from the obvious and significant damage to the victims, these supposed teachers cast a dark shadow over the entire spiritual field.

Even in the absence of such abuse, a teacher is still bound to attract criticism and even hatred from certain quarters. Indeed, no matter how impeccably you conduct yourself and how skilfully you wield the teaching, you're almost guaranteed to elicit the ire of somebody. I've seen this happen to my own teacher.

All it takes is for somebody to get annoyed by some remark or rebuke. Ego defence mechanisms fire up attack mode, and before you know it they've taken to social media in a bid to "cancel" you. Some can be ruthless in their pursuit, for they've projected a dark shadow and channeled all their own unresolved pain, anger and frustration onto a proxy figure.

As I've said, there are, sadly, many false teachers out there that should be held accountable—and, in the case of abusers and predators, prosecuted to the full extent of the law. The evidence may be plain to see when dozens and even hundreds of victims emerge to share their stories. When it's just a single person making an accusation, one should rightly be judicious. The fact is anyone can say anything about anybody in the anonymous back alleys of the internet. In the "post-truth" age, people can readily inhabit all kinds of alternate realities utterly divorced from empirical fact. The exponential rise of AI is going to make this even trickier as people increasingly struggle to discriminate fact from fiction.

One of the sobering things I've learned is that spiritual seekers are often wounded at some level. That was certainly true in my case. Indeed, for the majority of us, it was the pain of worldly life that propelled us onto the spiritual path in the first place. In some people's cases, it doesn't take much for them to project their pain, grief and personal dissatisfaction onto whoever happens to be visible. Sometimes, if a person stumbles along their own path, their unfortunate instinct may be to elevate themselves by tearing others down. I've seen that happen with former seekers; people who failed to progress on their own path, so they decided to lash out and attempt to bring others down in a bit to elevate themselves.

This, of course, is all just a part and parcel of the human condition. If nothing else, it demonstrates why relationships of any kind can be a minefield and why constant discrimination and discernment are prerequisites for navigating life. In an ideal world, you would be able to relax your guard in the spiritual arena, but that would be unwise when both teachers and students alike are subject to psychological blind spots, projection and transference.

You must keep your wits about you and remember the reason you're there in the first place. You're not there to be loved and given attention and validation by the guru. You are there for the teaching; the means of Self-Knowledge that will liberate the mind from dependence on all phenomenal objects—including the guru and the spiritual path itself! The idea is to get free and no longer even need a teacher or spiritual ideas. The spiritual path is not meant to last indefinitely. It has an end point, after which it is no longer needed.

It's probably no wonder I found myself hesitant to venture into teaching. I still don't really think of myself as a teacher. I'm just a writer and I share spiritual knowledge. I'm generally happy to just keep to myself and enjoy a quiet life, free of too many demands and ties. Yet, when the call of dharma sounds, it's only appropriate that we respond, for life is meant to be lived in service of God. As jivas, individuals, we each have our part to play. It's only right that we contribute as best we can in line with both personal and situational dharma. It really doesn't matter how well we do at it and whether our efforts are deemed a success or failure. What matters is simply doing what we were born to do as best we can and doing it in service of the divine. What better way can we live our lives?

A true teacher has but one objective; not even revealing the Self, because the Self, being self-shining and self-revealing, does that all by itself— but to remove our ignorance about the nature of that Self. Nothing more, nothing less.

"Contentment alone is enough. Indeed, the bliss of eternity can be found in your contentment."

Tao Te Ching

Satisfaction Guaranteed

Life continued quietly and simply for a couple of years. As my Self-Knowledge deepened, worldly things increasingly lost their allure until, after a certain point, I found I didn't really have any desires anymore. Oh, sure, there were things here and there; little things which made life a little sweeter; a trip somewhere beautiful, a new album by a favourite artist, a book to enjoy, or a cup of coffee and cake. Those were more preferences than driving compulsions, however.

Over time, any last hint of worldly ambition deserted me. They don't warn you of that when you embark on the spiritual path. Perhaps I had an unconscious assumption, at least initially, that if you "make it" spiritually, when you step back into the world, the world will kind fall at your feet and shower you all kinds of glory and riches. That wasn't what motivated me at all, but I think that's basically the delusion a lot of spiritual teachers are selling.

The reality is simpler and sweeter. When you know who you are, you realise that what you already have is utterly sufficient. So long as you have a roof over your head, clothes to wear and food to eat, you have everything that you need in life. Everything else is a bonus. When you've realised the incredible wholeness, fullness and, for lack of a better term, bliss of your own nature as pure Consciousness, nothing in the world can compare. All worldly pleasures are but proxies for the fundamental wholeness that is our own essential Self.

When you understand the nature of Reality, you realise that the world, as beautiful and terrible as it can be, is ultimately just a show; shadows dancing upon the wall; appearing real and tangible, but devoid of actual substance and inherent reality. Try though you might, there's nothing to actually hold onto. The creation is an ephemeral thing. Even scientists agree on that. If you take the most powerful microscope and use it to penetrate matter, the constituent building block of the material world, what you ultimately find nothing but empty space.

Like a wondrous light show appearing upon the screen of Awareness, it's undeniably fun to watch and immerse ourselves in, but there's no actual substance to the material world. Vedanta describes it as *mithya*, which means only apparently real. All that's ultimately real is *satya*, the witnessing principle; the Self, which has no beginning and no end and which illumines the creation, granting temporary sentience to all the forms; while itself remaining actionless, eternal and unchanging.

When this Knowledge truly sinks in, you find there's no longer any impetus to crave, desire and seek anything outside of yourself. Self is sufficient unto Self, for Awareness is utterly whole, complete and lacking in nothing. If you're not yet convinced of that—if you aren't completely satisfied with the wholeness that you are—that simply means you have a little bit of work to do integrating your Self-Knowledge. There's no shame in that, because the process takes as long as it takes, but I can guarantee that, in time, it will bear fruit and yield the liberation you seek.

For the longest time, I experienced a kind of seesaw effect. Like Jekyll and Hyde, I found myself shifting between truly knowing and feeling my own wholeness and Self-sufficiency to being pulled back into identification with the sense of being a limited, lacking person, driven by an array of conditioned attachments and aversions.

That's the way it tends to go for most seekers. It would certainly be nice if we could just click our fingers and shift our identification from the ego-self to the boundless Eternal Self.

But until Self-Knowledge reaches the tipping point and overwrites the old patterns of ignorance, the mind may remain something of a battle zone, at least at times. Indeed, that's why the Bhagavad Gita takes place on a battlefield and why Lord Krishna implores Arjuna to do his duty and fight. The Gita is not "pro war". It's pro standing up to ignorance and defeating the destructive ego patterns that have kept us bound in samsara for lifetimes. Commitment, perseverance and vigilance are key to winning this particular war, along with the mental qualifications outlined by Adi Shankara; namely dispassion, discernment, restraint of the mind and senses and the burning desire to be free.

For several years, I flitted awkwardly between identification with the body/mind/ego and identification with Awareness. At this point, you certainly need determination, grit and a healthy measure of self-awareness. Each time you get pulled into identification with the false self, as long as you're able to recognise what's happening, you can quickly course correct and reorient yourself to identifying again with the Self.

It's by no means an easy battle and complacency can ill be afforded. There were a number of times I mistakenly assumed, "Hey, I've got it—I'm finally *there*", only to find myself tumbling back into samsara whenever some particularly ingrained old pattern or attachment managed to reassert itself and take the mind hostage again.

If you stick with it, however, and resolutely keep your mind and heart fixed upon the knowledge, "I am the Self; I am pure Awareness", you'll find that, like any game, it gets easier and easier the more you play. You get wise to the pitfalls and dangers facing you and, bolstered by an equal measure of persistence and commitment, you make it to the next level, and then the level after that.

The real litmus test of whether your Self-Knowledge is

strong enough is a sense of a basic, fundamental satisfaction, contentment and wellbeing.

This satisfaction is completely independent of whatever might be happening outwardly in your world. The world could be falling apart around you, yet you find a strange and pervasive sense of contentment and "okayness" with everything. The reason is simple. You're no longer reliant upon the world of objects for your happiness. Your happiness is instead derived from knowing and experiencing the fullness of your own Being; the endless ocean of love, joy and stillness that is...You!

There's no losing it, either. A cloud may pass over the sky of your mind and cast a temporary shadow, but you dispassionately allow it to pass, knowing that nothing can dim or extinguish the eternally shining light of your own Self.

Words can't describe the blessed relief when you finally realise that, in spite of a lifetime spent desperately trying to fix up what you saw as a broken, imperfect self, lo and behold, you were actually completely whole, complete and perfect all along.

Oh, I don't mean the person you appear to be, which will always be subject to limitation and imperfection. I mean the *real You*; that boundless and imperceptible Awareness that animates the body, mind and senses. That's what you really are; the light and never the objects the light illumines.

The satisfaction comes from knowing that the light of your Self is constant, unchanging, ever-present and completely unaffected by anything in the world of form. This sense of satisfaction doesn't mean you'll wander around like a blissed out stoner all the time. I mean, there's nothing wrong with that, but it's not necessarily the most practical mode of living. In actuality, you may well function in a more integrated and effective manner than ever before. You continue to experience the play of the elements; your moods will change, thoughts will come and go (although most likely with far greater transparency than before) and life will continue its merry dance of duality, bringing experiences both pleasant and unpleasant.

Yet, through it all, you know that YOU are fine. The little jiva part of you may be having the worst day imaginable, but nothing ever touches the real YOU. As Awareness, you remain free and unaffected by pleasure or pain, joy or sorrow, desire or aversion.

Life just happens in you, through you, and you are that which witnesses. There's not even a witnesser anymore; there's just objects appearing and the ever present, self-shining Awareness in which they appear. That is the freedom.

It's not freedom for the person, as such, because the material part of us, this role that we're playing in the world of form, will always be subject to the laws of duality. There's no getting around that fact. The person is finite, limited and, like all things in duality, imperfectable. Liberation is accepting that and realising that what we truly are is always, has always been and will always be perfect and free; a boundless, all-pervading light without beginning and end.

One of the profound realisations along my journey was that, in light of this Self-Knowledge, I, as the person, was "off the hook"! I didn't need to keep trying to perfect myself, and no more striving to achieve this and that in order to be lovable and acceptable in the eyes of myself and others. I didn't have to justify my existence and somehow make myself worthy. I already *was* worthy at the deepest and most fundamental level; the level of pure and ever-shining Awareness. The same is true of all of us.

You might think of it as a kind of inner renunciation, whereby we renounce the false notion that happiness and fulfilment can be found outside of ourselves in the world of form. I believe this fundamental ignorance, this imprisoning lie, is what

Christians mean by "original sin". The happiness was always and ever in ourselves, in the splendour of our own shining Consciousness.

This renunciation doesn't mean that we turn our backs on the world, however. I knew I still had my part to play in life, as we all do. I had my dharma, my duty, to perform and it's only right that we have some way of contributing back to the field of creation. Nothing ultimately lives for its own sake. All things have a part to play in the functioning of the totality, and that is good. That's why I kept writing, not to mention creating music and visual art. I saw my work as a means of sharing the Truth of the Divinity inherent within us and of all life.

I felt compelled to create and contribute, but I no longer cared whether whether one person or one million people happened to buy, read or listen to my work. That was up to Ishvara, God, to determine. If a project didn't make money, I knew that was fine because Ishvara would bring money in some other way. I was doing my part, and doing it for the glorification of God rather than my little ego self; and, in turn I felt supported by the universe.

Not to say there weren't—and wouldn't be—problems. But I was fine; content living quietly and simply, doing my part, helping others when they asked for help, sharing words, music and art, being with my family, drinking fresh brewed coffee in the morning, going for walks with my beloved Spanish rescue dog, Cosmo, and appreciating the experience of life as it flowed through me.

That's not to say that life was always easy. Life has a way of testing us; almost as if to see just how integrated our Self-Knowledge, dispassion and equanimity happen to be. Between around 2018 and 2020, a couple of my closest family members were going through immense struggles—one of a physical nature, in the form of extreme chronic pain, and another in terms of emotional suffering. My own pain I can deal with, but I do find it exceptionally hard seeing loved ones suffer. While a true sannyasi [renunciate] would have severed all ties with family and, therefore, not be subject to such attachment, I knew that, for me, there was no walking away from such painful situations. I had to face them and allow the discomfort to be there and to move through me.

Life in maya isn't going to feel wonderful all the time. It's not set up that way. If we attach to the good and desperately try to avoid the bad, that may be a sign the ego's attachments and aversions are still subtly running the show. There's no freedom in that; only continued bondage. A healthier take is to embrace all that happens with as much equanimity and acceptance as possible, dealing with things as appropriately and objectively as we can, while knowing that beneath the flow of experience and changing forms, everything is always okay—it's all part of a divine perfection.

The "person" part of us is forever subject to duality and its vagaries of pleasure and pain, happiness and sadness, health and illness, birth and death. Self-Knowledge means we accept the flow of life, while knowing that, in ourselves (our true Self, that is), we are completely untouched by any of it. The sun shines upon the whole world, upon good and bad alike, and the circle of life continues in ceaseless motion; countless beings are born and die and entire civilisations rise and fall over eons of time. Although intimately involved with the entirety of all life, the sun remains untouched and unchanged by whatever is happening on the world beneath it.

In the same way, the Self is the source and the animating principle of all life, yet is never changed, hurt or modified by it in any way. Knowing this Self to be our essential nature is the ticket to freedom, even as the game of life continues.

"Let your life dance upon the edges of Time like dew upon the tips of a leaf."

Rabindranath Tagore

Karma

Confession. It's been impossible writing up my life story without frequent discussion of Vedanta. The reason for this is simple. Vedanta transformed the way that I see and understand everything. It enabled me to re-contextualise reality in a way that finally, *finally* made sense.

When I talk about Rory's journey through life I'm essentially talking about karma. Karma doesn't relate to the Self at all; the Self has no karma. But the jiva, the individual going through life, is both a product of and subject to karma. While the past couple of chapters have been devoted to the nature of the Self, this next section may seem to take something of a backward step as I switch back to the perspective of the jiva. After all, the Self never has any problems whatsoever. How could it when it's always and forever free, pure and untouched by time or limitation in any way? The jiva, however, the little pseudo-self, has rather a lot to contend with as it navigates life. That's because no being in creation is spared the push and pull of karma.

Karma is a Sanskrit word meaning "action". At a basic level, it pertains to the actions we undertake in daily life, whether grand and lofty undertakings such as starting a company or running for President or the more mundane actions like cleaning our teeth and feeding the cat. Karma also also refers to the results of our actions, so it really encompasses the spinning wheel of both cause and effect; everything that we do and everything that happens as a result of what we do.

According to Vedanta, there are three types of karma. Each have fancy Sanskrit names, but for the sake of simplicity, I'll refer to them as past, present and future karma.

Past karma encompasses the totality of all karmic imprints

accrued over the course of many lifetimes (and, yes, I do believe that while the physical body lasts but a single lifetime, the subtle body—the mind, intellect and ego—associates with countless other gross bodies much as the ocean is continually churning out new waves over the span of eternity).

From this bank of karmic debt, which exists in potential or seed form, a specific amount is apportioned to play itself out in any given lifetime. This might be thought of as present or "pipeline" karma. It's already on its way and it starts coming the moment we turn on the tap, which is to say, the moment we're born. This karma determines pretty much everything about our current lifetime—and, like everything in duality, will be a mixture of what we perceive as "good" and "bad". Some seem people to enjoy a better hand in life than others, but most of us experience a mix of favourable and unfavourable elements; the good, the bad and the ugly.

The third type of karma is the karma we create as we're going through this present lifetime; the seeds that we sow through our present day actions; seeds that will, in the fullness of time, take root and germinate.

It's karma that compels us to be born into the world of form. The ultimate aim is to resolve our karma; to achieve a cosmic balancing of the books. Until we attain that lofty goal, we remain on the treadmill of samsara. The way to escape this treadmill is to attain liberation or enlightenment. In simple and practical terms, enlightenment means to realise who and what we truly are and to shift our centre of identification from the body/mind/ego to the Awareness in which they arise. This breaks the bond of karma because there's no longer a "person" there to claim ownership of that karma. There will certainly still be the apparatus of a person and the framework of memory, personality and conditioning, but these are seen as impersonal elements incidental to our actual nature as pure, unconditioned Awareness or Consciousness.

The shackles of our painful misidentification with name and form are broken by the light of Truth, or Self-Knowledge. This Knowledge neutralises both the store of past karma and any future karma incurred in this lifetime. In the simplest terms, you attain freedom by realising that, "Hey, this is only just a game I got too carried away with. This karma never belonged to me in the first place because I was never actually this apparent "person" subject to time and limitation. I'm non-separate from the Self, from God; therefore, I have no karma!"

There's a catch, however. Isn't there always? While past and future karma are neutralised when you break free of false identification with form, the person you appear to be remains subject to the karma already set in motion for this particular lifetime. This karma has already determined the quality and configuration of your body, mind, personality and the basic experiences and proclivities that have shaped your life and character. This stream of present life karma will continue playing itself out until it eventually exhausts and the physical body expires. Our lives, at the level of maya, are all determined by the flow of karma.

We can learn to navigate life as best we can: working *with* our karma; accentuating the positives and manoeuvring around the inauspicious, but there's no erasing it entirely. It's there until it's no longer there. The sweet thing is that liberation grants freedom anyway because we are no longer identified with the body/mind/sense complex. This automatically grants us far greater objectivity and dispassion with regard to worldly happenings, for we see it all as the insubstantial, passing show that it is.

That's why, when we truly know who we are, we can be free and happy even if everything around us goes to pot. True and lasting happiness exists independently of whatever might be happening at an outer level. It comes not from objects, experiences and worldly attainments, but from the reflected light of your own innermost Self—something that, once found, can never be lost. Nobody is more grateful for that than I, for life at the physical level was about to become increasingly challenging, to say the least.

The shackles of our painful misidentification with name and form are broken by the light of Truth, or Self-Knowledge. This Knowledge neutralises both the store of past karma and any future karma incurred in this lifetime.

"All that we see or seem is but a dream within a dream."
Edgar Allan Poe

A Dream of Dark and Light

Not so long ago, a Vedic astrologer told me that I came into this lifetime with a particularly powerful configuration of karma: at once, both highly auspicious and highly challenging. From what I could grasp, there was some connection between the house related to my health and to moksha, or liberation. Health had certainly been a significant issue throughout my life. Yet, it was this limitation that afforded me the opportunity, the motivation and determination to turn inward and find the solution to life's existential suffering; to inquire deeply and find the truth of who I am and why I was here. I see that as a fair trade.

When we're only looking at things from the vantage point of the finite human mind, we are ill qualified to judge circumstances as either "good" or "bad". Indeed, life's greatest challenges and adversities often bestow the highest opportunities for spiritual growth and breakthrough. When I look back upon my journey through life, I see a tapestry of perfection even amid the seeming imperfection, and I would not change a thing.

I think I always assumed, however, that once I got myself sorted spiritually, somewhere down the line my health would improve and I'd be able to live a less constrained life. That has, so far been a false assumption. Contrary to what one might assume, the growing sense of wellbeing and freedom in my soul was not accompanied by an increase in physical health. In fact, between 2017 and 2019 I found my physical health deteriorating. This was in spite of the fact that, by and large, I lived a healthy, fairly yogic lifestyle. Karma, however, is karma, and, as long as the tap is running, there's no escaping what happens to be in the pipeline.

I'd been plagued by health limitations since childhood. I certainly had spells when it was less of a struggle, but I was generally kept on a tight leash due to exceptionally limited energy. Oh, I tried everything I could think of over the years. I wouldn't like to guess the amount of money I'd spent on various treatments, therapies and supplements. Nothing seemed to get to the root cause, however. Given that it all began when I was first diagnosed with and treated for cancer, I could only assume that either the disease or the treatment had left my body somewhat impaired.

For many years, I felt my physical limitations to be a mark of shame. I knew people twice my age or more who enjoyed far greater energy, health and stamina than I had. What could I do, though, that I hadn't already done? I soldiered on, putting my best foot forward and endeavoured not to complain because—well, nobody really wants to hear other people's complaints. At any rate, aside from immediate family, most people only saw me at my best and most functional, so few had any idea the price I would later pay for any significant expenditure of energy.

If I had it all to do over again, I'd be far kinder to myself and appreciative of my determination and spirit of resilience. If I'd given into things and allowed myself to succumb it, I'm quite certain I'd have been bedridden a lot of the time. Certainly, I was never that far from bed, but I had something driving me on, not only spiritually but creatively. A fire burned in my heart—even if, at times, its flames were dampened by worldly diversions and self-limiting beliefs and conditioning. I was an idealist with a deep rooted desire to contribute to the world in some way. That's why I soldiered on, even when it was a struggle to do much of anything and when all my efforts had failed to yield fruit. Although rarely able to do a fraction of what I'd have liked to have done, I did what I could. Sometimes life is just a matter of one baby step after another. Speed doesn't matter so much when sometimes the greatest accomplishment is simply to move at all.

Alas, by 2019, the fatigue was ever more debilitating and I was spending hours each day and night coughing up sticky mucus—and, worse, at times haemorrhaging blood. It had taken years to get a diagnosis, but I was finally diagnosed with a lung condition called bronchiectasis. Damaged airways predisposed me to infection and I'd likely been suffering continuous infections for years before they finally got to the root of it. Although an incurable and progressive condition, the diagnosis was a relief, for it went some way to explaining why I'd been so tired and sickly.

I spent much of that year finishing my book on the Bhagavad Gita. At the end of Summer, I had the pleasure of visiting James at his idyllic home in the Andalusian mountains of Spain. It was a joy to spend some time chilling with my guru. My favourite memory of my time there was sitting alongside James on the patio shelling almonds from the orchard while hearing about some of his adventures over the years in India and beyond. I was struck by just how much he lived and breathed Vedanta. From the moment he got up in the morning to the moment he went to bed, I'd see him writing to students, taking video calls, answering queries, working on books, videos and the website. I found his energy and dedication to sharing the Knowledge immense, one-pointed and utterly devotional. It was inspiring, and there was no motive at all on his part. After all, what is there to seek in the world when you already know you are whole and complete in your own Self?

That was also the time I realised that James wasn't seeing and relating to me as a person. Some little remark he passed made me realise that he was seeing and relating to me as the Self;

something you can rarely, if ever, expect from other people, even spiritual people. It's a wondrous thing when you realise that somebody sees you as you truly are, the highest and best in you, and isn't simply relating to the persona composed of name and form. It was certainly a week I cherished.

By divine grace, Self-Knowledge was taking deeper root in my own psyche and, as a result, life was grand. In spite of the physical limitations, I felt a steady inner glow of joy and contentment within myself. While I still obviously experienced the apparatus of the jiva, with its particular physiology, psychological framework and its odd triggers, my primary centre of identification rested with the Self; pure, simple Awareness. Desire and ambition had diminished to almost nonexistence and I no longer wanted anything from anybody. I only wanted to enjoy and appreciate the beauty of life and to do my dharma as and when appropriate.

I could, however, sense something in the air; a strange sense of unease rolling in on the Autumn breeze. I couldn't explain or understand it, but I definitely felt the atmosphere subtly shift. Whether it related to something personal or collective I didn't know. It almost felt like a pressure building up; a dam about to burst its banks.

One night, that November, I experienced possibly the worst nightmare of my life. I'm someone who rarely, if ever, experience bad dreams. My dreams are generally innocuous and pleasant, if I recall having any at all. This one, however, was anything but.

I found myself besieged by a storm of darkness. I was choking in it; drowning in it, all the while desperately trying to break free. It crawled over my skin and body, a virulent attacking void of blackness. It felt like some kind of psychic attack. I momentarily saw James and Sundari within a pocket of light, shining amid the eye of the storm. I knew that they represented spiritual truth and freedom. In that instant, I realised that, by reaching out and holding onto that truth and light, radiantly shining in the dark, I was free—free of the storm; free of the illusion of being subject to the laws of the phenomenal universe at all. I saw the entire realm of maya as but the play of smoke and mirrors; something hollow and illusory appearing as solid, tangible and, in this case, incapable of causing harm. The light—the light was our freedom; the knowledge of the Reality of God and the non-reality of everything else.

I nevertheless woke up feeling shaken. My nervous system was on high alert and it took a while to calm it back down. Yes, it was just a dream, but it felt portentous in some respects. I could sense that something was coming; something difficult; something that would push things to the limit. I knew the only way to get through it would be to remain fixed on the light.

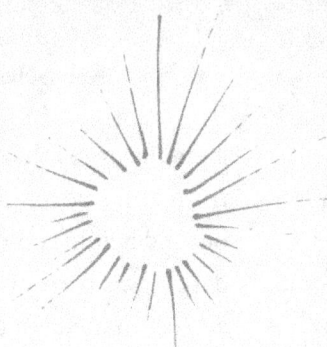

"The mark of your ignorance is the depth of your belief in injustice and tragedy. What the caterpillar calls the end of the world, the Master calls a butterfly."

Richard Bach

My Arjuna Moment

Although I'd had my lung condition diagnosed and had received treatment, it soon became clear there were other, more ominous symptoms. As well as recurrent anaemia, which the doctor simply treated with iron supplements, I'd been noticing bleeding when I went to the bathroom. No way to sugarcoat that one. It was infrequent at first and everything time I decided I'd go to the doctor it stopped, so I didn't go. That pattern continued on and off for a while.

I'm an optimist by nature. That can be a great trait, of course, but there may be times when optimism can work against us; when caution is the more appropriate response. I basically assumed that if anything was wrong it was only minor and would clear itself up. I was wrong. When I eventually did mention it to a doctor, by which time the bleeding had become constant rather than sporadic, she was horrified and told me that, "Young people are dying of bowel cancer because they're not getting symptoms investigated."

The moment the words left her mouth, I knew that things were serious. The thing with colorectal cancer is that by the time there are any significant symptoms the cancer, although slow-growing, has likely already reached an advanced stage. People over a certain age are routinely screened for this condition, but there's been an enormous increase in cases in younger people over the last decade or two and no one is sure why. There are certain risk factors, such as eating meat and being overweight, but I didn't and wasn't. In fact, since my college days, my lifestyle had been almost impeccably healthy.

I was booked in for a colonoscopy which was about as fun as it sounds. As they perform the procedure you can see the live video feed on a giant TV screen. "This is seriously the worst TV show I've ever seen," I joked. "Can't you change the channel?" Anyway, the culprit was soon identified and the whole screen was taken up by a large and bloody tumour. The word "tumour" wasn't used at that point, but it clearly was more than an "ulcer" and it really shouldn't have been there.

I took it in my stride, however. It was what it was, and there was no point in reacting emotionally because that wouldn't help anything. Afterward, the consultant couldn't believe that I wasn't getting upset and shouting and crying. He'd already learned that I was a writer and something of a spiritual teacher and, clearly impressed by my equanimity, said he would be checking out my books when he got home. It wasn't an act, either. I simply saw the situation with objectivity. Here was a problem, of which life provides many, and the next stage would be to explore solutions and, with a bit of luck, cures.

So began a flurry of further tests, scans, appointments and the wait for results—and it took several weeks just to confirm that it was cancer. Those few weeks were quite the test of mind management. My "get out card" was knowing that this situation wasn't ultimately real. Awareness, Consciousness, is the primary Reality and all the objects, forms and experiences that arise and subside in Awareness are temporary phenomena akin to dream forms. No matter what our challenges at the material level, the Self remains deathless and untouchable; the causeless Cause behind the world of temporary effect.

To those who doesn't understand Vedanta, which is the vision of saints and seers across all cultures and time, this may seem like an act of spiritual bypassing. Yet, to one who has lived and integrated this Knowledge into the depths of their mind, body and heart, it isn't an act of desperate aversion or denial. It's not an escape from reality, but, rather, a true meeting with reality as it actually is.

It's when the going truly gets tough that we get to test just how deeply integrated our Self-Knowledge is. Does our Self-Knowledge desert us the moment life throws a curve ball, or does that Knowledge sustain and protect us, enabling us to remain steady and stable even when confronted with what most would agree are objectively stressful conditions?

Perfection is unnecessary—which is just as well, too, because it's unattainable in this world of duality. Liberation isn't about becoming an emotionless Mister Spock, but simply being able to keep our centre and allow the raft of Self-Knowledge to carry us across the invariably choppy ocean of worldly karma.

When I did eventually hear back from the oncologist, I could hear the grim tone in his voice as he led with, "I'm afraid it's *not* good news." Not only was it cancer, but it had spread to my lungs and liver, with multiple nodes in both lungs. That was definitely not what I wanted to hear. I'd not long turned forty and assumed that I still had the second half of my lifetime ahead of me. Suddenly, I wasn't so sure. I didn't feel upset for myself though, for I knew this wasn't "me" anyway. I wasn't ill; the body was. I knew that I, the real "I", was fine and I'd simply do whatever was necessary and appropriate to navigate this sudden challenge.

It was my family I felt for and the worst thing I ever had to do was sit my parents down and deliver the news. I remember the look on Mum's face, and it's not one you would ever want to see on anyone you love. In all this time, I only ever cried one time and that was prior to telling my parents, because I was really didn't want them to have to go through such suffering.

In order to get through this, I resolved that there would be no complaining, self-pity or pessimism. Despite my laidback personality, I knew I had a warrior spirit inside of me. This was my Arjuna moment. I was on the battlefield and the opposing army, formidable in strength and number, was staring down at me. It wouldn't be appropriate for me to throw my hands up and concede defeat before I'd even fired a single shot. As it happens, colorectal cancer is one of the few cancers that can still be cured even at stage four. While the odds were stacked against me, it would have been premature to give up.

I now realised that living in this world is a privilege rather than a right. I'd simply have to work a little harder than most to retain my privilege. While fully cognisant that, as Awareness, I was absolutely fine and unaffected whatever happened to the body, I knew with some certainty that Rory's time wasn't up yet. There was still work to do. The fat lady may have picked up her songbook and started leafing through the pages, but she hadn't opened her mouth to sing yet.

With that in mind, I got up, dusted myself off and squared up to the antagonist; which was, as it happened, simply a bunch of confused cells in my body.

Me, on the other hand? I wasn't confused. I was resolute.

Let's do this.

It's when the going gets tough that we get to test just how deeply integrated our Self-Knowledge is. Does our Self-Knowledge desert us the moment life throws a curve ball, or does that Knowledge sustain and protect us, even when confronted with objectively stressful conditions?

"Pain is inevitable. Suffering is optional."

Anon

Dispassion and Dharma of the Body

Mercifully, by the time I was called to resume my cancer battle, Self-Knowledge had fundamentally shifted the way I saw and related to life. From the moment of my diagnosis, I had people remark at how "amazing" and "brave" I was and how, in the words of one friend, I was the "strongest person" she'd ever known. In actual fact, strength and courage had little to do with it. I simply knew who I was. I wasn't the body and I wasn't, therefore, affected by whatever happened to afflict the body.

Furthermore, I knew my body was not only *not* me—it didn't even belong to me. Like all things phenomenal, it belongs to Ishvara, or God. Me? I'm just the Awareness witnessing the flow of karma and responding as appropriately as I can, while retaining the dispassion that comes from dis-identification with name and form.

That's the freedom right there; not somehow trying to perfect your material life, because nothing in the realm of duality will ever be perfect. Freedom comes from seeing the perfection hidden beneath the veil of seeming imperfection.

Indeed, the liberation attained by Self-Knowledge isn't some magic bullet for perfecting the outer circumstances of your life. It doesn't confer everlasting health and physical immortality, nor an overflow of monetary wealth, nor all the hottest babes and hunks throwing themselves at your feet as you walk down the street.

Indeed, the karmic blueprint for your life—the "pipeline" karma as I call it—will, in all likelihood, remain pretty much as it was. If you're chasing enlightenment in order for all your dreams to spontaneously manifest and to somehow ascend into absolute perfection at every level of your life, I'm sorry to say you'll be in for a crushing disappointment. That's not what it's about at all. It's not about creating a better dream for yourself. It's about waking up from the dream altogether.

The change is not so much in how life unfolds, but in how we deal with and navigate the phantasmagoric world of duality. Ego-centred seeking and striving fall away when we truly know the indelible wholeness of our own being. With this comes a loving sense of dispassion with regard to the world of the senses. This dispassion crept up on me over time. It wasn't a quality I consciously sought to acquire or cultivate. It simply became my default mode of dealing with the phenomenal world—and that, as much as anything, enabled me to navigate the predicament of being diagnosed with stage four cancer with, on the whole, remarkable ease.

That's not to say the mind didn't throw up pockets of disturbance, because there is a degree of what I'd call human processing arises from such extreme circumstances. But I knew the futility of resisting what had already happened. Things are simply as they are, whether we might want them to be or not. I never once felt an ounce of self-pity because, as the outworking of karma, this was the just the way things were.

Rather than thinking of the cancer as some dreadful force trying to ravage my body, I saw it as a confusion over real estate. At a cellular level, I had certain tenants that weren't sticking to their property line and were trying to take over the entire town. These cells weren't evil; they were simply damaged and operating in an adharmic manner; in a way that was causing problems for every other cell and for "me" as landlord.

My case was a particularly difficult one due to the spread, but there were ways I could deal with it. It wouldn't be at all fun, as

I already knew from my childhood battle with cancer. I knew I could deal with it, however.

I learned to appreciate and lean into the subtle dichotomy of being surrendered to God on the one hand, while, on the other hand, taking up arms to fight for a more conducive outcome.

At the heart of life we find this inescapable seeming contradiction. Ultimately, everything is God; the good, the bad and the ugly. It's all divine and no matter what happens in the world of appearance, the Self that we are remains deathless and eternal. At the level of the relative, however, one outcome is invariably preferable to another, as determined by dharma. In life, it pretty much *all* comes down to dharma, which is why I find it a tragedy this most basic understanding is absent from most spiritual teachings.

That's why, when somebody me asked why I would bother to treat such an illness (as opposed to just yielding to it and letting the body just expire, I guess), the answer came down to dharma. As I explained in my response, we are each tenants of a body and dharma stipulates that we be good tenants:

The body is never "ours" to begin with. Think of it as a vehicle on temporary loan to us. Like all things phenomenal, it comes from and belongs to Ishvara. As tenants, we each have a duty to care for our body, to protect it and to enable it to heal and repair itself insofar as it can.

At the level of creation, everything is about dharma. The body has its dharma. It wants to live and be well, for life loves life and we instinctively know that it's a gift to be cherished and taken care of. That's why we have the miracle of an immune system and why the body instinctively steers us to what's good for it and away from what's harmful. We're each gifted with this wonderful apparatus and, as its trustees, part of our dharma is to look after that body, and to look after our mind as well, for that matter.

Life, being what it is, will forever throw challenges our way. While Vedanta gives us the Knowledge that we are ultimately free from duality and subject to neither birth or death, as long as we have the appendages of a body and mind, we still must navigate the maya world as best we can.

Some things we simply must accept, for Ishvara's decisions are often final. There are other times, however, where it's not only appropriate but necessary that we pick up our weapon, take a stand and fight. That's precisely the reason the Bhagavad Gita is set on a battlefield, both literally and metaphorically, and why Krishna repeatedly implores Arjuna to set aside his doubts and take action.

I've seen some critics of Vedanta, who perhaps know the basics but not the nuance of the teaching, argue that "Since we're all the deathless Self, why bother doing anything in maya at all? Why don't we just go throw ourselves in front of the nearest bus if it's not "real", after all?"

Such people, in promoting an impassive fatalism, are unwittingly adopting an adharmic viewpoint. While, according to the scriptures, the world isn't real in the sense that it is, much like a dream, ultimately just the play of Consciousness, that Consciousness is God. Therefore, everything in the world of maya is actually God assuming different forms.

That's why the gift of life should be embraced and lived with full participation, appreciation and commitment to dharma. The highest aspect of dharma is non-injury, so if a person were to willingly injure or destroy their body, whether through action or inaction, that would be tantamount to violence against God. That's why it would be wrong to throw away our lives and wilfully extinguish the body simply because we know we are ultimately unborn Consciousness.

Upon diagnosis, I was still relatively young, I had an illness that *was at least treatable and I also had dear family members who desperately wanted me to stick around. The diagnosis also brought a deep and immediate realisation of the true value and finitude of life in the phenomenal world. It's certainly a gift that should never be taken for granted, but cherished, maintained and, perhaps, if appropriate and necessary, even fought for.*

When you know that you're the Self, the realisation that the body is just a vehicle on temporary loan removes personal identification from it; and the existential suffering of samsara along with it. Like a car, if it's falling to pieces, you get it repaired or else it becomes useless to you. If it's beyond repair, fair enough, you'll be given a new one, but you shouldn't consider it a write off prematurely. The body is no different. It's a gift from God and should, therefore, always be treated with respect and cared for as the temple of Consciousness that it is.

My particular vehicle was in a dire predicament. I opted to trust the doctors because they were the experts in this field; they knew what they were doing, and I didn't. I view my doctors and nurses as instruments of God in action and I'm enormously grateful for their kindness, skill and judgement. I wasn't qualified to make the calls on my own, so I let them make the appropriate judgements for me while endeavouring to make myself as much an expert in the field as I could be, knowing that knowledge is power. I knew the treatment would be tough, but I'd gotten through it before and I knew I could do it again.

"The wise, awakened from the dream of ignorance, even though living in the body, know themselves to be apart from it. The ignorant, still dreaming dreams, identify themselves with the body."

Srimad Bhagavatam

Judgement, Compassion and Understanding

Things were at an advanced state, so it was important to stop the cancer in its tracks as quickly as possible. Accordingly, I began chemotherapy just as the coronavirus pandemic exploded upon an unsuspecting world.

I took each day at a time, which is the only sane way to live anyway. I had an "excellent" response to treatment and, over time, I educated myself in the therapeutic effect of diet, exercise, intermittent fasting as well as medications and supplements which target and weaken the metabolic pathways of cancer. There's significant evidence to suggest that you can give yourself an enormous advantage by approaching cancer from a metabolic standpoint. If you, or anyone dear to you, is affected by cancer, I recommend the work of Jane McLelland and suggest looking into the Care Oncology Clinic, which prescribes a regimen of off-label medications which aims to "starve" the cancer cells and make the big guns of standard treatment more effective.

My immediate family and most of my friends were such tremendous and unfailing support who would have done anything to help me. I feel tremendously blessed by all of them and humbled beyond words by their love and care, particularly my family.

Interestingly, however, a cancer diagnosis, particularly a bad one, has a way of whittling down friends. I found that even some friends I'd had for many years made themselves scarce rather quickly. It turns out this is a common phenomena for people dealing with cancer. Maybe it makes them uncomfortable or it's too much of a "downer", or maybe they have issues with their own mortality, but, for whatever reason, they either sever contact immediately or bit by bit. I didn't chase after anyone. If people wanted to slip out of orbit, I let them and instead focused on the luminous stars who did unfailingly light up my sky, of which there were many.

Something I found especially interesting was the judgement I received from some "spiritual" types. There's an undeniable stigma attached to cancer, perhaps because it often can be pinpointed to lifestyle and behavioural factors, although none of which applied in my case. These days, there's often a great overlap between modern spirituality and the "wellness movement", which more or less equates physical wellness with godliness. For some, peak physical health is almost viewed as the ultimate enlightenment. They see physical imperfection and illness as symptomatic of a "low vibration" or some underlying psychological, moral or spiritual deficiency in that person.

A couple of spiritual people I knew promptly dissociated from me. One such person tried to shame me for accepting conventional treatment and implied that if I had any courage at all I'd only use alternative therapies.

I have great value for alternative therapies. Their use, however, does not confer some moral or spiritual superiority. Furthermore, a person might have some degree of spiritual understanding, but that doesn't negate the laws of the empirical universe. While material science is of little, if any, use as a means of Self-Knowledge, it's still the best means of knowledge we have for understanding the empirical world—and surviving in it to a healthy old age. Science is, of course, open to corruption like anything else, but I would never assume that I know more than the experts simply because I see myself as "spiritual". I'm actually a big proponent of science and, furthermore, believe that if a person wants to get anywhere, they should adopt a scientific approach to spirituality and enlightenment as well.

When faced with life threatening illness, I wouldn't recommend a person goes to see, say, an acupuncturist or crystal healer in place of an actual doctor. As an adjunct, by all means, but you owe it to yourself to find someone who knows what they are doing. You certainly won't get more "spiritual points" by shunning mainstream medicine. Common sense remains essential. Its absence can and does cause many unnecessary deaths. Spiritual types naturally have a tendency to question and rebel against authority—and, spiritually, that can be the springboard that helps us to awaken from the dream of form. It must always, however, be accompanied by critical thinking and hubris kept in check by humility and pragmatism.

Fortunately, in spite of what anyone else might choose to believe, I knew there was nothing wrong with *me*; either with who I was as Awareness or as a person. I simply had some errant cells in my body. I didn't see anything personal in that. According to one doctor, in my case this was almost certainly the legacy of the cancer and treatment I'd had as a child. If anything, I was lucky to have been free for it for as long as I had been.

So, I refused to accept the judgement of others. I don't even judge my body for being sick. In fact, I've learned to have tremendous compassion for it—more so than I ever had at any point in the past. There's no "*me*" in any of it, either. I am not my circumstances, nor my body, mind or the content therein.

By divine grace, I'd reached a point where I no longer had anything to *get* from life. I was left with no real desires or goals, not even spiritually, because the very need to seek has resolved itself. I realised that if I do get to stick around a while longer, my only intent is to give: to serve and to share the Knowledge that set my mind free.

Everybody needs a best friend and mine is Cosmo, the rescue dog from Spain. (My face is red and blotchy in the above picture due to chemo treatment)

Blessed by my family, above in 1997 with my grandparents and below with my nephew and brother in law in 2022.

"The wise grieve neither for the living nor the dead. There was never a time when you and I did not exist, nor will there come a time when we cease to exist."

Bhagavad Gita

There is No Death

I have zero fear of death because I know, beyond a trace of doubt, that death does not exist. I've known that my entire life, even before I really understood why. For me, it's a deep and unassailable knowing. Death pertains to form, so the body is obviously out of luck, but the essence of what we are—pure, unconditioned Awareness or Consciousness—transcends form. It can never die because it was never born in the first place. Like the light illuminating a room, this Self exists everywhere, pervading and revealing all things, yet is contained and affected by nothing.

The unassailable logic of Vedanta reveals that the subject cannot be perceived as an object. Anything perceivable by the mind and senses, including the mind and senses themselves, cannot *be* the Self. What we are is the eternal subject; the illumining and ever present Awareness that serves as our carrier of reality; the light by which all forms, gross and subtle, are apperceived and known.

For this transcendent Self, which is the basis of all that we perceive and all that we are, there can be no death. While forms may come and go like rippling waves upon the boundless ocean, the Awareness underlying form always remains. Universes come into being and fade into oblivion, but the underlying continuum of Universal Consciousness remains untouched, unmovable and eternal.

Death, therefore, poses no problem for the Self. It can only ever be a problem for the jiva, the person living in maya; and even then, the problem only exists as a thought in the mind. Mind and body are but mirrors allowing for the reflection of a sun that will never set or cease.

The idea of having advanced cancer and an uncertain future was is an unsettling one for the mind, as you might imagine. Fortunately, I recognised this was just thought. A thought poses no problem unless we invite it to supper and allow it to move in and take up residence (which it most certainly will, given the chance). If it gets too comfortable it won't only hang around, it'll multiply and, before you know it, it's running the show. It's far easier to manage thoughts as they arise. Don't let them get too comfortable. If a thought arises that disturbs your mind, simply zap it! A cool technique I discovered for zapping thoughts was to simply identify the offending thought and declare "Not helpful!" It'll take the wind out of its sail like nothing else.

I admit I'd assumed, as we generally do, that my body would live an average lifespan and that, as a result, half my lifetime still lay ahead of me. God willing, it may yet be. Earlier this year my oncologist said he doesn't know if I have three months, three years or even potentially thirty years. The same is actually true of everybody, however. Everything that is born will die and we know not when.

The future is God's business, not ours. Krishna clearly states in the Bhagavad Gita that as long as we fulfil our dharma as best we can, everything else is ultimately taken care of for us. We need only look around to see a greater hand at work in all things; and it's the same sentient force that creates the stars, galaxies and planets and causes rivers to flow, clouds to form and stars to twinkle. There's an undeniable intelligence at work and it's guiding all things.

I've found that the more that we surrender to God, the more we experience the sense of being held by God. Ultimately, surrender isn't even an act of will or intent. It's the product of Knowledge; of knowing the Divine nature of Reality.

Why worry about anything? That which is Real can never be

harmed, injured or lost, for its essence is eternal—and that which is unreal doesn't exist in the first place.

Knowledge of Reality doesn't arrive alone. With it comes peace and freedom from fear. The truth is, we are eternal *Being*! No matter what's happening in the world of appearance, and how threatening it might seem from the level of body and mind, it cannot touch us; the Reality of what we are. Maya conjures a dreamlike mirage like a cloud passing over the sun. Even if heavy cloud appears to dim the light, casting darkness upon the land, the sun shines regardless.

Life is unquestionably tough when, subject to ignorance, we identify ourselves with the finite vessels of body and mind. In fact, it can be a veritable torture chamber. But when we know what we really are, and we stick with that Knowledge until it overwrites the mind's old operating system, guess what happens? Everything flips. The phenomenal is revealed as mere appearance and the conceptual ego identity seen as the hollow sham that it is.

We come to realise that it's all fine—even the bits which don't seem so fine. Certainly, that doesn't mean that we don't take action in the world to create a more conducive outcome for the jiva. But we know with the entirety of our being that, regardless of what's happening at the level of karma, what we are—specifically, the Consciousness shining in our deepest heart and the hearts of all beings—is always and ever free.

"The one Eternal Self dwells in the hearts of all beings. That one Existence is seen as many beings just as the moon appears to be many when reflected in many vessels."

Srimad Bhagavatam

The Ultimate Aim of All Spiritual Teaching

Prior to Self-Realisation, life certainly had its moments of wonders and joy, but it could also be a painful struggle. A friend once remarked that I probably had it much easier than most because I was so laid back and "together". That wasn't always the case, however. In fact, I got hit pretty damned hard by the samsara stick. My challenges included significant health limitations, difficulty finding and having the confidence to commit to my dharma, feeling as though I didn't fit into the world or culture around me, spells of depression and anxiety, unresolved karmic patterns, trying to find wholeness through often less than healthy relationships and, at the root of it all, a tremendous sense of inner lack and self-doubt.

I felt that I had to justify my existence to the world, and that I was doing a lousy job at it, too. I judged and berated myself for not measuring up to the illusory ideal of perfection conditioned into us from childhood onward. It's only when I look back over journals written ten to twenty years ago that I remember the extent of my inner torment. I can now see that the suffering was all rooted in thought; specifically, thoughts of ignorance, born of the failure to recognise and appreciate what I actually am.

Then, by God's grace, Vedanta appeared as the culmination of a long spiritual search. It revealed to me that actually this ego identity had nothing to do with who and what I am; that what I am is already perfectly whole, pure and complete; and that I didn't need the validation of anyone or anything outside of me in order to be free. But for the thoughts wreaking havoc in my mind, I was already free and I always had been.

Committing to the path of Self-Knowledge, I gradually and painstakingly hacked through the chains that bound me; chains forged by erroneous thought and the mass hypnosis predisposing human beings to identify with the aggregates of body, mind and ego. It certainly didn't happen all at once or in some grand flash of light. Rather, over the fullness of time, I began to reorient to a far vaster and freer understanding of who I am: Awareness free of all thought, limitation and impurity.

That's the ultimate aim of all genuine spiritual teaching: relinquishing the dream of personhood to the knowledge that we are one with the Eternal Self, the nature of which is *Sat Chit Ananda*—Existence, Consciousness and bliss.

The Upanishads declare the highest and most direct expression of universal Truth as *Tat Twam Asi*; "I Am That". This realisation, the scriptures state, liberates the soul from continued rebirth into the world of form. It does so by not only extinguishing our deeply ingrained attachments and aversions, all of which are driven by an inner sense of lack, but by divesting us of our false sense of doership and ownership.

We come to realise that, as Awareness, we do nothing, have nothing and own nothing. This entire creation is a play of form, a dance of karma, governed and directed by Ishvara, the Divine Mind. What we perceived as the "outer" reality is actually a projection occurring within us. Like a dream at night, it may seem totally immersive and both glorious and frightening in equal measure. It is, however, nothing but a cloud arising and passing by in the changeless substratum of Awareness. What we truly are, the essence of our being, is not to be found anywhere within the dream. Rather, we pervade the dream as the changeless Light revealing all experience.

When this Self-Knowledge shifts from intellectual understanding to ironclad certainty, we reclaim the liberation that is our birthright. We free the mind from its false identification with name and form; with the aggregates of body, mind, ego and the entire universe of concepts and thoughts that so readily imprison the mind.

The attainment of liberation is life's highest goal. While participation in the game of life is mandatory, a lifetime spent entirely in pursuit of worldly desires and attachments is a meaningless one. While there's no doubt great beauty and joy to be experienced in the game itself, the wise know that our ultimate goal is to achieve freedom from the chains of samsara. When at last it's "Game Over" for the pseudo-self enmeshed in samsara, what remains is a blissful reclaiming of our essential oneness with the Eternal.

"Eternal Self", digital artwork circa 2010.

"Those who depart from this world without knowing who they are or what they truly desire have no freedom here or hereafter. But those who leave here knowing who they are, and what they truly desire, have freedom everywhere, both in this world and the next."

Chandogya Upanishad

A Free Mind

Why seek liberation? Most people don't. Even among self-proclaimed spiritual people, it's rare to find someone who is actually, genuinely committed to attaining enlightenment. A great many spiritual types are unconsciously looking to feed rather than transcend their ego and feel special by "being spiritual". No judgement; we've likely all been there at some point. The question is whether we get to the point where we're genuinely serious about the whole thing; when we're ready to truly *get real* about enlightenment.

Depending on the state of a person's mind, getting there will likely to take a lot of work. It's not for the indolent or the easily discouraged. You need to fully commit to it. There are no half measures. I was lucky in that my karmic path provided me the time and space I needed to get serious about this. Even though worldly distraction frequently certainly set in, sometimes for long periods, I rarely missed a day's meditation in twenty five years. By and large, I had time to devote to the study of spiritual knowledge, culminating in my discovery of Vedanta and the grace of finding a good teacher.

Alas, there's nothing glamorous or sexy about the path of Self-Knowledge. Let's face it; regular people will think you're crazy or, at best, a bit of a kook. It can be isolating because, to an extent, it's necessary to isolate—or, at the very least, insulate—yourself from the world, lest you continue to be swept away by the endless distractions and storms and stresses of worldly life. You need to free up as much time as you possibly can to study, learn and then, crucially, to exhaustingly contemplate that knowledge and apply it to the mind until such time as the mind finally gets the memo.

Then there's the mind itself. For many, if not most, the mind gallops about like a wild horse. Until you rein it in, it'll drag you here, there and everywhere, driven by all kinds of desires, aversions and lifetimes of conditioning and ignorance. Like any kind of training, all that ultimately does the trick is persistent effort and resolve.

If the mind is reasonably under control and you have been blessed with a legitimate means of Self-Knowledge, there comes a time when you begin to experience the fruits of its application. Swami Paramarthananda calls Self-Knowledge the great "shock absorber". The best antidote to the stresses of life is to know who you truly are. This knowledge will grant you a rock steady sense of well-being, equanimity and security quite independent of external factors. When you're no longer reliant upon objects and "things" for your happiness and security, you naturally develop a sense of dispassion.

That doesn't mean you become cold and uncaring. I, for instance, still very much care about people, animals and the planet itself. It doesn't mean the body and mind always feel great, but there's a sense of wellbeing present even when things are difficult outwardly. While there are bumpy moments, I feel the sense of being carried through life; as though I'm not doing anything myself, but simply letting life flow through me while I enjoy the show.

I do enjoy life, too, more so than I ever did in the past when I was constantly worried about what others thought of me and whether I would ever actually "amount to anything" in worldly terms. I now live with a state of gratitude and perpetual wonder. Each day is a blessing filled with countless things to enjoy and cherish. I still have preferences, of course, but no great desires and no real fears. Free of any kind of ambition, I am content with life as it presents itself.

I've learned that even once you begin experiencing the fruits of Self-Knowledge and know that it's working for you, you should never consider your journey "done". That's one reason it's bad spiritual etiquette to declare yourself "enlightened" and then set out to make sure the world knows about it. It's far wiser to keep your head down and continue purifying and refining the mind and psyche through the consistent application of Self-Knowledge. My recent health issues have actually been a great blessing in that regard, for I have used the challenges to purify my mind and weed out some problematic layers of old conditioning and patterning.

Even when a newfound sense of freedom arises, you can bet there will still be layers of ignorance-based conditioning, reactive impulses and psychological triggers which require careful examination or, at the very least, vigilance. Your primary job is to keep the mind pure, steady and focused upon the knowledge that you are Awareness. The knowledge itself does the work, steadily and over time, although it may take years or even decades for it to fully integrate into every nook and cranny of the mind, intellect and heart. Even when a tipping point is reached, I've found there's an ongoing process of deepening in which Truth is ever more reflected by every thought, word and deed.

The more you rest your mind in its Source, pure Awareness, the more you come to experience a lasting sense of peace, steadiness, stillness and desirelessness. In time, all sense of seeking falls away. That may, at least initially, be quite disorienting if you happen to have spent most of your lifetime as a spiritual seeker. Along with it, worldly ambition dries up, along with any compulsive need for romantic relationships, the pursuit sensory pleasure or outer validation. What tremendous liberation that is! Life tastes infinitely sweeter when you're no longer focused on seeking love but content in the delight of simply giving it.

There comes a great sense of transparency to the jiva part of us. Body and mind function as before, but the removal of identification renders them far "lighter" and more translucent. I've certainly found my mind has become quieter and, while I experience pleasant emotions such as love, gratitude and joy, it's not often that I experience what I'd describe as "negative" emotions. If I do, it may manifest as a kind of instinctual tension in my gut, or a pang of anger when I encounter cruelty and adharma, or when some old psychological wound gets triggered.

Generally, a sense of contentment and basic well-being pervade my heart now; a sense of satisfactoriness, for lack of a better word. It's a strange and subtle sweetness, for even amid the sorrows of samsara so rife in the world, I'm aware of God shining through form as an eternal, illuminating light; much as consciousness pervades the entirety of a dream at night—and, because of this, it all feels all right.

When my mind is particularly calm and settled, I feel illumined from within by a wondrous sense of joy; the joy of existing, of simply *being*. It's a bliss beyond description. Nothing in the world of the senses can compare—nothing but genuine, pure love, which, I've come to realise, is the essence of what we are as Consciousness. It's not "out there" in the world, even if that's where we've spent a lifetime seeking it. This love, this joy, exists within us and *is* us. Nothing exists apart from it. It was there within us the entire time, hiding in plain sight.

Self-Realisation leads to a kind of Divine vision, for you begin to perceive, at first in glimpses and then for more sustained periods, the Divinity in everything, everywhere. After all, if God is Infinite, and it cannot be anything less, then it must already be *here and now,* in this very moment, all around you. There can't be anything it is not. That Infinite, ever-shining Light is already present and attained. All separation, and all discord, sorrow, lack and grief exist as maya's delusion; nothingness masquerading as reality, with no reality, no inherent substance of its own. The only thing that is real is the Light revealing the worlds of sense and form and this Light can never be eclipsed or extinguished.

Liberation is rather like waking up from a dream within the dream. The dream itself continues unfolding, but instead of being completely pulled in by all its dramas and horrors, you now simply observe it with a sense of wonder. You continue to play your part as before, knowing that the dream is just an appearance happening within you and something that can never touch or harm you in any way. After all, you absolutely transcend it! You are the Light in which the whole show is, for a time, happening. To understand the true nature of Reality is to be free of it.

In the words of Rumi:

"Wake up! This world that you dream has nothing to fear."

"Each day, the first day. Each day, a life."

Dag Hammarskjold

Savour Each Day

Life becomes easy when you allow Ishvara take care of things. Of course, as an instrument of God, we must continue to play our part as and when appropriate. Fortunately, the burden of doership is lifted when we see ourselves, at the level of personhood, as just a cell in the great cosmic body of Ishvara, functioning by an innate divine intelligence of which we were never apart.

These days, my physical health remains precarious. Whereas most people don't have to do much to stay alive other than eat, drink and sleep, I have to work a little harder to retain a functional body. That's just the way it is. I believe I still have some karma to fulfil and, until that is accomplished, the body will be around even if it requires a lot more maintenance and care than most.

Fortunately, what I lack in physical energy, I have gained in less tangible inner wealth. Whereas some chalk it up to me being "strong person", I really just approach life with a combination of dispassion and appreciation. When my mind is still, I see God everywhere I am: in the singing of birds, the shining of the sun, the presence of a loved one, the affection and all round awesomeness of my dog, Cosmo, the sound of silence or music, and even in a sip of fresh brewed coffee. Life is a feast of wonder and richness if we just have the ability to see and appreciate it. Nothing is ever lacking in spite of whatever the mind might claim, for each moment presents itself as a veritable universe of *purnam*, or fullness.

I found that having cancer again stripped away everything inessential, from outdated friendships and unworthy goals, to any remaining pockets of vanity or ego. I remember taking a hair trimmer and shaving my hair before it could fall out as a result of the drugs. It almost seemed metaphorical. Everything inessential was just sheared away, swept up and thrown out. And I was fine with that.

I recall lying on the sofa one night, recovering from a chemo treatment, accepting the various discomforts and pains and realising that I was absolutely fine in spite of the condition of my body. The sun was shining in as the sky became a kaleidoscope of pinks, orange and yellow. I was listening to my favourite singer, Elizabeth Fraser of the Cocteau Twins. The simplicity of that moment; lying, resting, watching the sun and sky, listening to Liz's sublime singing, was just heavenly. Eventually the sun disappeared behind the neighbours' rooftop and that, too, was perfect.

The only appropriate response to life? Gratitude. Always gratitude.

Any difficulties and limitations I've faced along my life's path have served to strengthen me and fired my resolve to break through the binding chains of samsara. As of writing this, I was told nearly four years ago that my body was ridiculously ill and the prognosis beyond dire. I took this an opportunity to test and strengthen my Self-Knowledge and to smooth out some of the rougher edges of my personality and some lingering shadows of past trauma.

As a result, I can now say, with complete honesty, that I've never been happier and more at peace in myself. The key to getting through life is to turn the challenges into victories by turning within and purifying the mind and heart, and nothing purifies like the alchemical fire of Self-Knowledge.

Only a clear mind can adequately reflect the resplendent light of our own Self. Such a mind, which can be cultivated through commitment to dharma, the practise of karma yoga, devotion, meditation and the deep contemplation of Self-Knowledge, is a mind freed from excessive want and ego-driven desire.

Life is no longer about getting what we want. It's about finding the deeper part of us that's forever *free* from want—the part that simply shines in changeless splendour. This inner light is the only remedy to the veiling cloud of ignorance that keeps us desperately bound to worldly objects and oblivious to the fact that we are in actuality, in our heart of hearts, already free.

I now appreciate life in a way that I never did before. Every day, every moment, is a blessing and gift. Whereas, in my younger years, I saw life as a burden and something to escape from, I am now joyfully aware of the preciousness of simply being existing. So, take nothing for granted! It is all a glorious and gratuitous blessing.

I do want to make it clear that I have not written this book to make myself, as a person, seem special or exalted in any way. In fact, there's nothing special about this human being, who, like all beings, is simply doing his best to navigate life. If anything sets me apart from the average person, it's that I have a radically different take on the nature of Self and Reality; and that's the gift given me by Vedanta. This Knowledge catalyses a deep and lasting sense of peace, freedom and fullness regardless of what's happening around us in the world of form. It worked for me and I know it can work for anybody else as long as the appropriate effort is expended.

The gift of Self-Knowledge is shifting your identification from what you appear to be to what you truly are: the vast, unfathomable, self-shining and ever present Awareness or Consciousness that is without birth, death or limitation.

This Self isn't to be found elsewhere; in some distant, exalted dimension or plane of being. The Self is everything everywhere—not only the Intelligence shaping and sustaining the cosmos, but its very heart, substance and essence.

Sometimes people are inclined to dismiss the path of Jnana Yoga, or Self-Knowledge, as some cold and intellectual exercise. With the sustained practise and integration of that Knowledge, however, I guarantee that you'll come to feel and experience the all-pervading divinity of all things. We don't just realise the divine Self within us, but everywhere; in and around us and shining in the heart of all beings, even if, often times, seemingly obscured by less than divine behaviour. The phenomenal world exists as one immersive magic show of fathomless proportions. Fortunately, much like the magician's saw, nothing can actually harm us when everything when we realise it is all simply divine slight of hand.

Life without Self-Knowledge is generally characterised by pain and limitation. Life with Self-Knowledge, however, makes you love and appreciate life for no reason other than the joy of simply existing. Gloriously, you no longer require validation from any external source. I believe that's the secret to navigating this world: getting to that place of Wholeness in your own Being where you want nothing *from* life, but simply delight in what you can contribute *to* life.

My physical form continues chugging away as best it can. I am owed nothing so I am simply grateful for what comes. Compared to others in the same boat, I seem, by God's grace, to be doing very well although it does require treatment to keep at bay. My creative spark remains undimmed. Since my treatment began, I have managed to release or re-release soon to be five books and three ambient music albums composed, performed and produced from scratch (I release music under the name

Ajata). I am committed to sharing Vedanta and the liberating power of Self-Knowledge with all sincere seekers of Truth. I see it as my way of paying back the gift of life and the resources that have been spent keeping this vehicle in working order.

There's no end to an autobiography. So I see this as an open-ended conclusion. I may well come back and add to the book or refine it every now and then. I don't feel there's a whole lot more can be added in terms of the spiritual side of things, however. After all, I am the Self (and so are you and everybody). I've always been the Self and will always be the Self. Only misidentification with form, whether the world of gross forms or the subtle world or thought, can make it seem otherwise. There's nowhere to go now and nothing to get. The Self is always there, always present, always shining and without beginning or end.

Ultimately, I live each day as it arrives. Each is a gift to be unwrapped with reverence and savoured from dawn until dusk. I find enormous pleasure in the simplest of things. When you finally step off the samsaric treadmill, you find yourself with no real desires, so you're invariably satisfied with whatever the moment brings. At the very least, you are alive and, I hope, have food to eat, shelter, clothes and company. What more do you need to be grateful? As long as you draw breath you are blessed with the opportunity to realise the divinity of your own Self and of all life in each and every moment. How great is that!

When we surrender to the sweet fullness of Existence and manage to keep the mind relatively calm and tranquil, each moment can be a lifetime in itself, overflowing with wonder, innocence and delight.

Content with life. Gran Canaria, Spain, 2016.

When we surrender to the sweet fullness of Existence and manage to keep the mind relatively calm and tranquil, each moment can be a lifetime in itself, overflowing with wonder, innocence and delight.

"If the doors of perception were cleared, everything would appear to us as it is: Infinite."
William Blake

A Meditation on Awareness (What We Are)

I am Awareness.
I cannot be contained,
Nor located in any particular place.
I have neither beginning nor end.
Existing as a seamless whole,
I pervade all things and nothing.
I am a self-shining light; illumining and revealing the worlds of form.
I am the contentless whole in which all appearances arise and subside
Like waves upon the ocean of eternity.
Things come and go in Me;
In this all-pervading, beginningless, ceaseless ground of Being.
That is my direct experience.
I am the space in which all things have their being.
All objects, gross or subtle, can be directly seen and experienced
But I, as Awareness, cannot.
All objects have a location in space and time
But I, as Awareness, do not.
I cannot be seen, touched, smelled, tasted or heard.
I cannot be experienced as an object.
Yet, it is because of Me that all objects can be experienced.
Whereas objects possess clearly defined boundaries
I find no boundaries or limits to the Awareness that I am.
As Awareness, I am not subject to the laws and limitations of physicality.
As Awareness, I have neither inside or outside, neither up or down,

Neither pleasure or pain.
As Awareness, I exist without effort.
I am an eternally shining light without beginning or end.
As Awareness, I am Here, Now; actionless and ever present.
Without any effort, I illumine all things,
Yet I am not available as an object of illumination.
As Awareness, I need and lack nothing,
For I am without limit, without edge or boundary.
Free of hunger or thirst, desire or aversion,
I just AM—This, Here, Now.
Transcendent yet immanent,
I just AM—This, Here, Now.
Untouched by anything in the worlds of form,
I just AM—This, Here, Now.
Containing all yet contained by nothing,
I just AM—This, Here, Now.
As pure Awareness, unmoving and eternal,
I just AM—This, Here, Now.

"Emancipation", acrylic ink artwork from 2001.

"With life as short as a half taken breath, do not plant anything but love."

Rumi

A Meditation on Jiva (What We Appear To Be)

I scrawled the above words one day while in meditation focusing upon my nature as Awareness. I didn't think about what I was writing. I just sat in contemplation and allowed the words to flow through me. Although written in first person perspective, I could just as easily have used second person, for each sentence applies equally to you, and to all beings. After all, it's one Awareness illumining all beings, much as the one sun shines upon all the world.

Afterwards, I got up, made a cup of tea and let the rest of the day flow by, appreciating the wonder and joy of being alive; Awareness shining through maya and appearing as a person named Rory—and as my dog, my family and everyone and everything else around me. Isn't life a marvel?

"What a wonderful life I've had! I only wish I'd realised it sooner."
Colette

What I've Learned In Life

One of the tragedies of being human is that we grow up hypnotised by the values of a hyper-materialistic culture. We are conditioned to seek happiness and fulfilment entirely outside of ourselves, through the acquisition of money, possessions, social status, romantic love and whatever else.

There's nothing wrong with any of that in and of itself. Certain stages of the human lifetime will naturally be dominated by the pursuit of security and wealth, relationships, career, family and so on. Our fundamental mistake, however, the one at the very root of samsara, is the idea that we can find lasting happiness and fulfilment through objects alone. I came to this realisation relatively early on in my life.

When we seek happiness we expect that happiness to last. If it doesn't last, it isn't really happiness at all, because it comes with the bitter sting of subsequent sorrow. The problem with seeking happiness in the objects of the world is that all objects, all forms and experiences are in a state of constant change and flux. A world of duality is a world of contrasting opposites. Try though we might, we cannot experience up without down, pleasure without pain and happiness without sorrow. Sooner or later, the object we've invested so much time and energy into acquiring with fail to bring the same rush of joy and pleasure. In time, it may even become a source of displeasure and suffering. There's simply no getting around this fact. Seeking infinite happiness in a finite world is a recipe for endless frustration and grief.

That led me to one of the most important realisations of my life. I came to see that *the love, joy and wholeness that we seek is never to be found outside of us.*

That may be hard for most people to understand. It seems counterintuitive. After all, it certainly seems that when you get or experience something that you like, the good feelings are coming from that particular object or experience. But whether it's a promotion at work, winning the lottery, meeting the guy or girl of your dreams or whatever else tickles your fancy, these things don't actually *bring* happiness in themselves.

What they do is tap you into the joy and wholeness already existent within you. When you get something you want, the mind is temporarily satisfied and this suspends the bitter cravings of lack, want and desire we're otherwise all too familiar with. In one spacious instant, you are free to enjoy the reflected light of Consciousness shining at the core of your own mind and heart; something you may rarely experience due to the mind's agitation and the concealing and projective powers of maya.

This shining Consciousness is the very Heart of our being, described in the Vedantic scriptures as Sat-chit-ananda: Existence, Consciousness and the Bliss of limitlessness. The joy we seem to experience through the fulfilment of our desires and attachments was actually already there, deep within us. The object of our desire was only ever a proxy; enabling us to feel good—which is synonymous with feeling God—by tapping us into the boundless and inexhaustible well of wholeness, peace and freedom at the core of our being.

Life has different purposes depending upon a person's age, duty and culture. The Vedas outline the first three main life pursuits as security, pleasure and dharma, which means to do the right thing in any situation and to be true to our own nature. Life's final and ultimate pursuit is liberation, or enlightenment.

Liberation is the full integration of the Knowledge that we *are* what we seek; and that, contrary to appearance and assumption, what we are is not a limited, lacking little ego-person, but the pristine pure Consciousness or Awareness illumining and enlivening a temporary body and mind. The body and mind are but mirrors reflecting the light of Brahman, God, or the Ultimate Reality. That's the great secret of life, right there.

Even those who don't think they believe in God spend their lives pursuing the Infinite in all kinds of ways. The fervent materialist will seek God (wholeness, fulfilment, bliss) through money, ambition, possessions, and perhaps drugs, sex and various other hedonistic pursuits. Each may seem to be a portal to bliss, but the happiness is always temporary. A wise person will eventually concede to this fact. The foolish or indignant, however, will spend an entire lifetime trying, in vain, to somehow extract Infinity from the finite.

A lot of people still harbour an outmoded and misunderstood concept of God as a cantankerous old man sitting in the clouds casting judgement upon His creation. God, however, is something far more immediate and familiar: the very light of our Consciousness itself. That light is always there, no whatever what turbulence happens to be rocking the body/mind/ego with all its attachments, desires and aversions, beliefs, concepts and emotions.

The light of Consciousness forever shines, regardless of whatever is going on at the level of maya. That's why, at heart, we are always free. Nothing can ever touch the light that we truly are; not any experience, any fear, pain, hurt or even the crippling burden of a distorted egoic self-concept. Like the sun always shining above the clouds, Consciousness is forever free, always available and without limit or boundary.

Very few have the ability to fully grasp this, even among spiritual seekers. Only sincere and committed enquirers have any way of processing this understanding. To the average person, it will seem nonsensical and irrelevant. This Knowledge, however, is the key to alchemising life and turning the lead of worldly sorrow and limitation into the gold of perfect Divinity.

Compared to many, I don't feel I have achieved a whole lot materially in this lifetime. That really isn't why I am here, however. My life path has been an opportunity to use limitation and adversity to turn within and realise the light within myself and within all beings.

That's the key to this game of life.

Integrating this Knowledge into the core of my psyche was far from an overnight job and I stumbled repeatedly along the way. It led, however, to a treasure far beyond compare: the discovery of an unending ocean of inner peace, contentment and joy that none of the vagaries of worldly life can ever rob us of. Even though a thought or emotion might cloud the sky temporarily, this light can never be lost because it is the true essence of what we are: pure Consciousness wearing the temporary sheaths of a body and mind.

While I wasted a few too many years seeking love and validation from others, the ultimate realisation was that I already *have* and *am* everything I'd ever sought.

What's more, the person I thought I was existed as nothing but a concept in my mind; a set of conditioned thoughts, reactions, desires and fears, capped with a name: in this case, "Rory".

Now, I admit it's a mighty strange way to end an autobiography, but, in ultimate analysis, there's no such person. It's all just story. I don't see myself as Rory now. My centre of identification is just Awareness functioning through a body and mind. Even when you find yourself having to take action, and pick up your bow and take to the battlefield like Arjuna, life flows quite by itself if you let it. All that needs doing—all the words spoken, actions taken and thoughts thunk—happen automatically by virtue of Consciousness enlivening a body and mind. What a wondrous thing!

It may not happen overnight, but with repeated application to the mind, Self-Knowledge brings with it an unspeakable sense of relief, freedom and joy. There's still obviously a world of names and forms appearing before these eyes, and certain likes and dislikes and conditioned patterns cycling through the mind, but it's all fine because I know it is all God. The light just shines as all forms and beings dance to the tune of karma.

Bodies come and go, lifetimes pass by in the blink of an eye, stars are born and die, universes come into creation and dissolution, but the light of Awareness, always present in all beings and universal in nature, shines endlessly. There's no birth for it and no death, and all limitation is but the product of maya and is, to Awareness, as insubstantial as a dream. Awareness always remains and can never be touched, tainted or harmed in any way.

This Knowledge brings liberation. We pivot our centre of identification from the conceptual ego identity to the Awareness in which it arises. Only then do we taste freedom from seeking, freedom from lack and freedom from having to continually manipulate the outer world in order to satiate our desires and cravings. In spite of whatever might be sprouting in the endlessly fertile field of karma, the reality is that you, the *true You*, is already and ever free.

"You are pure Consciousness, the witness of all experiences.
Your real nature is joy. Cease this very moment to identify
yourself with the ego."

Adi Shankaracharya

Be Free

Enjoy life and celebrate the world!
We each have a part to play, so give what you can.
Cease, however, looking to the world for your happiness,
For anything gained outside of yourself is subject to loss.
Some people are capable of loving you, others are not.
The human ego, driven by desire and aversion,
Is characterised by limitation.
Love all regardless, without expectation of return.
Such love reveals the Unity of all beings.
With mind and senses automatically
Hooked onto the world of form,
Almost all seek their happiness outwardly—
In things, events, possessions, experiences, and
In boosting the ego by whatever means necessary.
Some desires are attainable, but many are not.
No lasting joy can be derived from temporary forms
Forever subject to change and dissolution.
Now, hear the secret of the Ages!
To find lasting freedom, turn within
And seek That which seeks.
As the experienced mediator will attest,
A sufficiently stilled mind will yield
Immeasurable peace, equanimity and bliss.
These are not jewels added to you;
But the innermost essence of what you are.
A precious human lifetime can pass by in a flash;
So seize this moment and realise your highest destiny.
Commit to taming the restless mind,
Bound as it is by desire, fear and attachment.
With steadfast spiritual practise, free your heart

And take to the path of Self-Knowledge.
Find out what you truly are beneath form and appearance.
Look within and learn that you *are* that which you seek.
The greatest treasures can never be taken from you—
Love, peace, fulfilment and joy.
These are intrinsic to your nature and
Not the product of worldly acquisition.
The Light contains your experiences and transcends them.
While body and mind are limited and time-bound,
The Light revealing them has neither beginning nor end.
That Light of Awareness is *You*.
Fix your mind upon It,
Break the spell of materialism and
Know the part of You that never changes
Even as the world around you perpetually dances.
The Kingdom of God lies within
And you alone have the key.
Commit to a life of freedom;
Of pure resolve and inner alchemy.
Turn the lead of worldly bondage
Into the gold of liberation
By seeking the Light within;
By seeking the Light you are—
A Light that shines
Beyond all things on earth,
Beyond us all, beyond the heavens,
The very highest heavens...
The Light that shines in your Heart.

"The supreme truth of Vedanta, the highest knowledge, is simply this: I am the Self, pure Consciousness; that which shines within all beings. As Consciousness, I am formless like the sky, unchanging, ever pure and changeless."

Avadhuta Gita

Further Reading and Listening

For more information on Vedanta

Bhagavad Gita - The Divine Song (A New Translation and Commentary) by Rory B Mackay
An accessible and clear rendering of this timeless treasure is accompanied by a comprehensive commentary following all eighteen chapters. Inspired by thousands of pages and hours of talks by some of the most brilliant teachers in the field, this book serves as not only a manual for the spiritual path and daily living, but a course outlining pretty much all the fundamentals of Advaita Vedanta. A German translation is also available courtesy of translator German May.

How to Attain Enlightenment and **Essence of Enlightenment** by James Swartz
The first is the book which changed my life by introducing me to traditional Vedanta. It holds an enormous place in my heart. The second, "Essence of Enlightenment" covers many of the same topics but is written in a simpler manner. Both beautifully unfold the core principles with tremendous skill and precision. James had a range of other books available through ShiningWorld.

Vedanta: The Big Picture by Swami Paramarthananda, edited by Rory B Mackay
This beautiful little book is a succinct overview of the core concepts of Vedanta and is based upon transcripts of talks given by one of the best living teachers of Vedanta; Swami Paramarthanada of Chennai. Published by ShiningWorld.

Avadhuta Gita: Song of the Liberated Soul by Rory B Mackay
A translation and commentary of one of the most loved Vedantic texts, this is a beautiful pocket size book with brief commentary on select verses. Its powerful and pithy verses are ideal for meditation and deep contemplation.

Other books by Rory B Mackay

Tao Te Ching: The Ancient Book of Wisdom by Rory B Mackay
All 81 verses rendered with clarity and accompanied by commentary unfolding the key message and themes of this beloved ancient text.

Eladria by Rory B Mackay
A visionary sci-fi/fantasy novel with a metaphysical twist; a fast-paced, action-packed story using fantasy and fiction to deliver a vision of the deeper aspects of life and reality. First published in 2013 by Cosmic Egg books; a second edition is now available from Blue Star Publishing.

The Key of Alanar by Rory B Mackay
My favourite book; one I spent decades working on and developing. Another metaphysical sci-fi/fantasy novel exploring the nature of life, death, purpose, grief, redemption and ultimately enlightenment; all set on a vivid fantasy and spanning no less than 10,000 years.

Music by Rory Mackay

Ambient electronic music composed and performed by Rory for relaxation, meditation, study, sleep and general enjoyment.

The Stars Do Dream (2019) — Album by Ajata, released by Astropilot Music

Fragments of a Dream (2019) — EP by Ajata, released by Astropilot Music

Into Bliss (2021) — Album by Ajata

Dreamlight (2022) — Album by Ajata

Immortal (2023) — Album by Ajata

Eladria (2023) — Soundtrack Album by Ajata

Om Tat Sat.

"If you have only one breath left, use it to say thank you."

Pam Brown

www.ingramcontent.com/pod-product-compliance
Lightning Source LLC
Chambersburg PA
CBHW070054110526
44587CB00013BB/1414